Bryan Charles Waller

The Twilight Land, and Other Poems

Bryan Charles Waller

The Twilight Land, and Other Poems

ISBN/EAN: 9783337251802

Printed in Europe, USA, Canada, Australia, Japan

Cover: Foto ©Thomas Meinert / pixelio.de

More available books at **www.hansebooks.com**

THE TWILIGHT LAND

AND OTHER POEMS.

THE TWILIGHT LAND

AND OTHER POEMS.

BY

BRYAN CHARLES WALLER.

LONDON:
GEORGE BELL AND SONS, YORK STREET,
COVENT GARDEN.
1875.

TO THE MEMORY OF

BRYAN WALLER PROCTER

HIS NEPHEW

INSCRIBES THESE POEMS;

OF WHICH DURING HIS LIFETIME HE HAD

ACCEPTED THE DEDICATION.

LET THEM BE, IF NOT AN OFFERING,
AT LEAST AN ELEGY: IF NOT A TOKEN OF AFFECTION
FOR THE LIVING, AT LEAST A TRIBUTE
OF RESPECT AND ADMIRATION
TO THE MEMORY OF THE UNDYING DEAD.

DEDICATION.

AWAKE, wild Harp of Twilight, with the eve,
   And like a lone wind through bare autumn boughs
Sigh thou among thy strings in music strange,
Soft as new-fallen snows, and as the sea
Fulfill'd with white unutterable woe:
For he is dead, our eldest child of song.
And on the face of this our labouring earth
There is one glory less, and from the gloom
Of earthly skies one pure and silvery orb
Has evermore departed, like a strain
Of deathless sweetness, which the wandering soul
Has heard in dreams, and seeks through waking days
With weariness of hope, in vain for ever.

Awake thee then, wild Harp, and through the wastes
Mourn echo-like, till every trembling leaf
Of every tree, and every murmurous stream,
And every quivering herb through which heaven's breath
Flits soul-like, catch the burthen of thy song,
And every mountain peak grow grey with cloud,
And every valley weep thick mist of tears:
For he is dead, and we that with sad feet
Toil through life's solitudes, shall hear no more
Sweet spirit-songs about us,—no more see
Bright forms of cities and of palaces,
Cool flashing of full fountains, which at sound
Of his now silenced voice, as by a spell,
Made all earth's deserts blossom like the rose.
Arise and utter forth thy soul in sound;
Yea, breathe upon the void of air, and break
The clasping stillness with a wail of woe,
For now thy ghostly tones should float and steal
Like sorrow through the spirit, and dispel
The dull sick voiceless heaviness of pain:—
For he is gone whose clear melodious song,
Like plainings of the nightingale at eve,
Fired the dead silence of the wilds with soul,

And hung upon the tresses of the dawn
Till day like night was hush'd, night glad like day.

   Lament thou too, Euterpe, through the groves
Of orphan'd Helicon, for never more
About this weary wilderness of world
His soul shall roam in harmony and move
Upon its listening vastness, as of old
God moved upon the waters;—never more
His songs shall cheer men onward, as the voice
Of one that from a cavern's blackness calls
Across dull gaping rifts and sullen streams
To those that follow fearfully, and tells
Of crystal halls begemm'd with fairy pearls
And grandeur of dim subterranean aisles:
For he is fled beyond this narrow sphere,
Past the weird shadowy Border-Land where Time
Merges upon the dark eternal realms,
Where broods the heaviness of wakeless sleep,
And thin white images of many dreams.
And where among the countless worlds of worlds
Blows there the wind that from those slumberous
      shores
Shall waft us but one echo of his strain?
What Argus eye shall pierce that sightless gloom,
And see the laurel green about his brows,

And all his face illumined with the light
Of deathless song, or marble-still perchance
Sunk in strong sleep that knows not any dream?
Lament thou, O our Mother, by the stream,
And by the forest edge, when dusky Eve
Clasps hands with duskier Night, and by the sea
At dawn of day, and by the mountain tops
Robed thick with raiment hoar of ghostly pine,
And by the yellow valleys red with grain,
For he is fled, O Mother, like a dream
Scatter'd in foam upon the crags of morn!

Yet died he not as he that dies unknown,
Whose place being empty but one moment's space
Shall reck not of the perish'd human weed
Now faded, nor remember him at all,
Nor form nor fashion of his face for ever:
For while the quenchless flame of song shall burn
Starlike from age to age, his luminous soul
Shall float within the halo of its sphere
An effluence of Infinitude, and shine
Among the central radiance, like a gem
In mid Elysium of a virgin's hair.

His soul soars heavenwards far beyond our ken,
Yet may we follow on Thought's wings and see

The Eternal City's starriest gate unclose,
And one stand watching, waiting, till his feet
Light on the golden threshold, and his hand
Clasp hers once more,—once more his brightening
   eyes
And all his face grow tender as of old,—
Once more his lips breathe forth a father's love
For her that was his daughter:—lost awhile,
But now regain'd in lands where sunnier skies
Smile peace on souls that shall not sever more.

Hush then thy wail, wild Harp of Twilight
   Hours,
Wail not for him, for surely he is blest!
Wail for thyself if thou wilt wail;—thy voice
Is lost as in a forest, and the hand
That was the wakening spirit of thy frame,
Has now forgot its cunning:—hang thou mute
Upon the cypress by the sullen stream;
Perchance a wind at times shall wander by
Shaking the sombre leaves about thy strings,
And rouse the phantom of some dreamy lay,—
But now, thy mournful tribute paid, be still.

CONTENTS.

	PAGE
THE Twilight Land	1
The Death of Baldur	21
Witch-Song on the Death of Baldur	48
A Lay of the Life of Man	53
Song of Sleep	63
Three Years Ago	70
The White Bird	76
The Loneliness of Power	81
Lines suggested by a Picture	88
La Belle Dame sans Merci	93
Ariadne Relicta	97
Maidens	102
The Vision of Ezekiel	103
The Scarlet Letter	107
Past and Present	114
Love and Wine	117
Maud	119
Wandering Fires	120
The Owl	122
The Bat	123

CONTENTS.

	PAGE
A Valentine	125
Song. In the Forest	128
Song. Lost Love	131
Life	133
Singing	136
To One Departed	138
Love's Comparisons	140
To —— With a Camellia	142
Sonnet. To the Sister Nightingales	144
Clara	145
The Garden of Love	146
Little Flo Colburn	148
My Loves	157
Lady May	160
The Days of the Years of our Pilgrimage	162
Morning, Noon, and Night	164
Desolation	166
A Farewell	169
New Year's Song	172
Song	175
A Flower Phantasy	177
The Scald's Death-Song	183
Finis	187

THE TWILIGHT LAND.

THE TWILIGHT LAND.

THERE is a life other than this on earth,
    Round which the shadows of the
        Future hang—
    There is a land far far away in silence,
On whose dim shore Eternity's vast flood
Dashes its billows, where the air is dark
And sad as with o'erlooming destiny;
Where in the glimmering light among the trees
Dim shadows flit about, as night's still birds
Fly noiselessly through darkness, when the day
Is done, and midnight stretches through the void.
It is a land where we sometimes in spirit
Journey on ghostly wings, as the lone bat
Glides through the churchyard on some autumn
        eve,
Making with leathern wings a murmuring,

That seems a lullaby to the calm dead
Sleeping below: it is a land where all,
All that is dear or hated here on earth,
All that is good or vile, bright, fair, or foul,
Shall mingle one day in a multitude,
As here on earth; though then earth's busy scenes
Shall have pass'd for ever, and before our eyes
Loom the long shadows of the Twilight Land.

The Twilight Land! within the Future's haze
Mistily hid, lieth its dim dark shore:
Our bark, now sailing over Life's fair ocean,
Nears day by day its mystic shapeless strand;
Friends vanish in it, and its silence broods
Upon the tomb that holds what once was man,
And merges in its own infinity
The glow-worm beams of glory and of power,
As the bright rainbow with its aery hues
Blends slow and slowly with the gleaming sky,
Tint after tint dissolving quietly,
And mingling with the vast ethereal blue,
Which closes o'er it as the waters deep
Close on a stone within some lonely lake,
Where man is but a wanderer like the bird.—
Yea, as a flower whose many-colour'd leaves
Expand towards the sun and gentle rain,

Whose petals shine with dewdrops numberless,
Within whose pearly cup the bees at dawn
Gather sweet nectar,—even such is man:
He blooms awhile upon the kindly earth,
Awhile puts forth his odours to the wind,
Awhile with beauty glads the restless eye;
Then, like the flower, he fades and vanishes,
Or like the grass that on the housetop grows,
Whereof no mower gathers kindly store,
No binder-up of sheaves his bosom fills,
Save hungry Death, that plucks it by the roots,
And bears it hence, a wither'd weed and dry,
To lie forgotten in the Twilight Land.

 I stand alone at even in the meads,
Watching the stars break from their canopy,
Like chaste love dawning in a maiden's eyes,
While the white moon above me throws her beams,
Silvery with spectral light, upon the trees,
And streams that dance like wavy threads of light,
Murmurous with music such as might beseem
Some elvish dance of fairy fable old.—
The woods around are silent, hush'd, and still,
While the old mansion of grey frowning stone
Stands in the starlight like a wizard rock
 In some enchanted isle: and my thoughts wander

As do the moon's cold beams through endless space.
Oh! ye bright stars shining in heaven's vastness,
Oh! thou wan moon that hold'st thy ceaseless way
Through the quiet night, imaging Eternity,
How do I envy your unruffled calm!
My spirit stirs and heaves to burst the bounds
Riveted o'er it by this earthly clay;
Would I could soar to your infinity,
And sing as never man yet sung, or else,
As other men around me, rest content
To live in earth alone,—it may not be.

There is a something stirring in the breast
Of some few men on earth; 'tis hardly known
To the dull crowd who live but in the flesh;
Which compasseth our thoughts with halos bright,
As 'twere the glory of Eternity
Bursting the mystic veil 'twixt Space and Time,
And shedding rosy light as of a dream,
Or of the wizard sunset's crimson'd hour,
On all we see, or know, or hope for here.
Think ye these few are happiest or best,—
Think ye their life is but a glorious dream
Of things so lovely that they may not be
On this side immortality? Ah! no.
They see as with a prophet's eye, they live

Conscious how low is e'en their loftiest thought
Compared to that they know is fair and good.
Great Knowledge and Great Sorrow, mighty twins,
Come hand in hand to man, and oft we see
The child of wisdom hides an anxious soul
Beneath a placid and unruffled brow.

   I stand alone, and thoughts which many a time
Come thronging through the mind rise up again,
Solemn as is the silence of the earth,
And grey light yielding step by step to night.
Methinks the hour that stands 'twixt dark and day,
That hour when moon and sun together shine,
Both indistinct yet still perceptible,
One waning to the horizon in a cloud
Of purple halos lit with streaks of gold,
The other in a veil of pearly mist
Shining as doth the snow-flake crystalline
In the young morn,—methinks this hour doth speak
Of that great Border-land which intervenes
Between this world and that which is to come:
Methinks there is a meaning in the calm,
Which tells of turmoil past, and rest beginning,—
And Life seems happier, Death less terrible,
The great Plan clearer, whose one end is Love.

I stand and meditate, and now my thoughts
Half shape themselves into realities,
These into words, and so I muse and write.
Reader, wilt follow to the Twilight Land
As far as flesh may follow? Thou shalt go,
I know, hereafter, but shalt not return:
Yet follow now the windings of the song,
And in imagination thou shalt see
The curtain rise which hides the Land of Dreams,
Nor tremble when thou seest the gate is Death.

Years hurry on until the latest comes,
Days pass away, and nights close over them,
Until there comes a day when the dim eye
Looks its last farewell on the woods and skies,
Lingers on well-known features with a love
Deeper because it cannot choose but go,
And leave love, life, and happiness behind,
Like the forgotten vesture of the moth,
To crumble, while the deathless spirit flies,
Not as the butterfly, through golden skies
From the low earth into ethereal bliss,
Soaring aloft with many-colour'd wing,—
But as the screech-owl, when the morning sun
Bursts through the East, to duskiest cavern's gloom
Hastens, and like a shameful thought of sin

Hides its dazed eyes from the detested dawn:
Thus flies man's spirit from its mortal home,
Leaving the dimpling splendours of the sea,
The wealth of beauty spread o'er earth and heaven,
The faces that were dearer than them all,
With one last agonizing pang, which tears
The heart like months of torment;—vain, ah vain,
Thou mayst not stay,—the voice of child and wife,
The sweet discourse of friends, the father's care,
The mother's yearning tenderness, can last
But the poor moment while thy panting breath
Trembles as yet within its tenement,
And when 'tis gone thou hast them then no more.

One hour, and all that thou canst wish is thine,
Friends, riches, life, the dearest boon of all;
Another comes, and not the populous world
Cramm'd with the hoarded treasures of old Time
Can aught avail thee; poor and desolate,
Naked and stript of every earthly joy,
Yet free alike from earthly care, thou goest
To be a phantom on a phantom shore,
A mockery in a land of emptiness.—
Yea, it is deathly silent in the grave,
And yet perchance 'tis peaceful;—rest so deep

Should yield a respite from all waking woes,
And Pain and Pleasure be alike unknown.

Man lives below a few sad tearful years,
And sows the wind, and reaps as he has sown;
And the far echoes of the perished days
Of youth aye crowd around him, as he walks
Through rough and smooth, through sun and
    storm and snow,
On to the churchyard and the silent mound
And mouldering headstone under yew-tree's shade,
Where pillow'd in the quiet of the grave
His form shall rest for ever,—lull'd perchance
By the wild cry of curlew 'mong the hills,
The call of moor-bird, and the bleat of sheep;
Or 'mid the hurrying city's ceaseless din,
Less blest in its last resting-place, alone
Voiceless amid the roar of thousand tongues,
Fall into dust, nor dream of absent soul
More than a ruin'd tower of bygone times
And men long dead, that were its lords of old.

Sleep,—rest in peace, ye dead! afar from all
The tinsell'd mockery of this hollow world;
Ye lie so very quiet in your graves,
That one might think that ye had found at last

Calm if not happiness within the veil
That hangs between us and the Twilight Land.
Yea, one might deem that on the dreamy sea
Beyond Life's shore ye float with halcyon wing,
In the grey light beneath the moon, that shines
Among the spectral clouds that overhang
The dawnless night we call Eternity,
Whilst we are battling with the angry foam
Among the breakers on the waves of Time,
Like some frail skiff within a whirlpool's grasp.
Sleep, sleep! your rest is won, your haven gain'd,
After life's storm comes quietness as deep
As is the blue of that all-clasping vault
Where shines the sun, and blinking stars that ride
Like wandering souls adown Infinity.

What is our life?—a thing of straws and dust,
A transient vapour clad in hues to which
The colours of the gay Ephemeris,
The vows of woman, and the faith of man,
The rose's opening blush, the lily's bloom,
The worldling's fleeting wealth, the passing cloud
Are lasting as a massy granite wall
Beside the gipsy's hut of sticks and mud.
Childhood is sweet; it passes like a bird
Wending with winter to its tropic home:

Youth sweeter still,—" Oh stay, ye radiant hours,"
We murmur, but the hours relentless pass.
Manhood is bright, but ere we look around
We see the coffin and the charnel-house,
We hear the solemn requiem of the dead,
And as from sleep awake on other shores,
And dreamlike pass into the Land of Dreams.

Oh! happy they whose minds can never stray
Beyond the hour; happy but yet not blest,
For in the midst of all the inward war
The souls of those that are not of the world
Soar upward ever through the snows of air,
Above the mist that hides the things that be,
Where Time and Sense are lost within themselves.
These touch a truth which must for ever lie
Hidden from all the howling dregs of earth,
Who know but what they hear and feel and see:
These reach a height to which no flesh can climb,
These penetrate a mystery beyond
The blunted senses and earth-fetter'd brain
Of human beasts who live like ox in stall,
And fatten like the hog on filthy husks.
These flourish like the bay-tree, till the wind
Of Death sighs through their boughs,—and where
  are they?

Unloved, unwept, they vanish into gloom,
With none to say, " God bless thee for thy deeds ;"
With none to whisper sadly, " Fare thee well ;
While thou wast here thou didst a glorious work,
Thy silent life sent forth a nobler strain
Than solemn anthem from deep organ swell,
Or choir of harpstrings swept by angel hands :
Friend of the poor and helpless, Fare thee well."

The toil of man for knowledge or for gain,
The poet's verse, the statesman's eloquence,
The weird harmonies of musician's pen,
The stone-transforming sculptor's magic art,
The blended tints of that eye-poetry
Which hangs like life from out the picture frame,
End with our day, and then the twilight comes,
When we can work no more, and what is done
For good or ill remains behind, while we,
Borne like a drifting snowflake on the blast,
Pass into the dim precincts of the dead.
And what we there shall be can no man know :
Imagination like a wandering wind
Roams through the void, and seeks to find a name
For thoughts which none can utter ; there be shapes,
And sounds, and words, beyond man's power to tell.

It may be that the spirits of the gone
Speak to our souls although we hear them not;
But poet's verse and artist's canvas fail
To give a body to the bodiless,
To lend a form to filmy shadow scenes:
And so it haps that, as in this my song,
The Unexpress'd is greater than the Told.

It may be that ye trust in fables here
To shed a light upon the trackless gloom,
It may be that ye deem that after death
There comes not twilight but a blaze of dawn,
A key to every earthly mystery,
As says the Faith that preaches of the Fall,
And the Redemption of the race of Man
From a deserved eternity of doom.
Vain tale! we live without a light to guide,
A hand to succour, or a voice to cheer;
We know not what shall be, nor have we aught,
Compass or anchor, for our misty voyage,
Save Reason, which the fool would say "Forego,"
To trust in wandering stars and dangerous gleams
From the false lighthouses of creeds, which lure
Their votaries on to sunken rocks and sands,
And helmless there abandon them to roam
Without a beacon on a shoreless sea.

There is one Purpose, could we see its bent,
There is one Law by which all things that be
Immutably are govern'd, and its end—
What is it but that mystic Kalon, sought
By many a sage of ancient heathenesse?
What is it but that aspiration known
To loftiest souls, which teaches them that they
Are form'd for—what they know not,—something higher
Than mere brute life upon a brutish earth?
What is it but that universal Plan
Of the Creator, when He bade the spheres
Revolve by Law, and move in harmony
With all the thousand voiceless melodies
Of air, and sea, and grove, and stream, and hill?
And so we trust that in the dim hereafter,
Or be it dawn or twilight, noon or night,
The thread of that great scheme whereof this life
Is, as a something tells us, but a part,
Will not be lost, but taken up again
And woven into one completest whole,—
One spotless fabric free from rent and stain,
One work of which that never-ending strain
Wherein is blended every smallest sound,
Which each minutest organism that breathes
Within the limits of created orbs

Sends up to Him who made and fashion'd all,
Is as a bar in some vast symphony.

  Our life must end, and be it dawn or dark,
The substance or the shadow, who shall tell?
Or what Death shows, or what within his caves
Of more than subterranean blackness hides,
We know not:—and to speculate were vain,
As was those virgins' bootless toil, condemn'd,
So says the myth, to fill with slippery water
A vessel without bottom. All we know
Is that we are, and not what we shall be.
Yet Reason lends the lamp, which needing else,
Our souls like marsh fires o'er some dreary waste,
Dancing amid the dismal fens, would stray
Aimlessly on without or goal or guide.
But She from faintest footprint on the road,
Or stillest whisper in the ear of thought,
Gathers some light, makes some fresh progress,
      knows
Something that yesterday was mystery all;
For thus She argues:—If the web be whole
Of that great texture of existing things,
Through which we travel onward to the end,
That God who bids us thread the labyrinth
Will not withhold the clue from him, who seeks

Not by insensate rushing here and there
To stumble on the pathway, but by mind
To read some little of the mind of Him
Whose will, albeit oftentimes obscure,
Is after battle fought and conflict won,
Grim desert traversed, mighty river passed,
To lead His creatures to a Land of Peace.
And in His works themselves solution lies,
For nought that e'er was formed is made in vain,
And that creative Hand of God, whereby
The never-ending span of world on world
Formed out of nought was stretched across the
    void,
Which on some peaceful night we view, and call
Earth, heaven, planets, stars, the Universe,
Hath penned in these a mighty volume filled
With mysteries and with wonders, infinite
As their Creator:—every orb that keeps
Its course through Space bound by unchanging
    Law,
That knows not deviation through the roll
Of countless eons,—every germ of life
That lives its little being in a day,
Are eloquent beyond the power of speech
To him whose eye can see, whose mind can grasp
That Revelation which the Maker writes

On every work, or be it great or small,
Yet perfect still and beautiful, beyond
The power of man to equal;—he who knows
In smallest dusty atom of the air,
In humblest beast, in leaf of lowliest herb,
To trace the hand of Him who made it good,
Is wise beyond the myriads whose sole trust
Is old wives' story, lighter than the wind,
Or smoke wreath of a taper in a storm.

 Therefore let Reason guide, and where she leads,
Careless alike of censure or of praise,
How steep soe'er the path and dark the night,
Let us press onwards, upwards, heavenwards,
In firm and filial confidence in Him
Whose light is in our minds, whose changeless
  will
Orders our steps, whose all-embracing love
Would we but trust it where we cannot see,
Nor vainly importune Omnipotence
To change His own immutable decree,
And in our blindness think to teach the hand
That made the spheres, how better to direct
Our own weak way, far surer than we deem
Would bring His perfect work to perfect end,
And ere our wondering consciousness could grasp

Out of the seeming chaos one fine thread
Of tangled purpose, all perplexities
Smoothed by consummate wisdom, one by one
Would yield without our effort, and the skein
Of Life, which not the less is Providence
Because it is as God unchangeable,
Unravel into deftly blended Plan;
And out of maze of wildering intricacy,
Which to our eyes was anarchy supreme,
Evolve the changeless harmony of Law.

  Thus far my song has wandered, like a bee
Through sunlit pastures carpeted with flowers,
Into a wild unpeopled wilderness,
Where lost amid the vastness of its theme,
Like a faint thought that scarce has touched the
    brain,
It fades into the Nothing whence it sprung.
I may not lift the shadowy curtain, hung
Before a shore whence none that goes returns,
Or but in phantoms:—o'er the Twilight Land
The evening shades fall back again, and now
My thoughts, which ghostlike roamed in other
    worlds,
Turn home again to earth and earthly things.
And so until we pass the mystic bourne

'Twixt Time and Space 'twill ever be,—for man
Within the viewless portals of the dead,
Within those shores where nought has form or
    name,
Only in dreams can sojourn, and when these
Depart, his spirit like a demon called
Back to his torture, wakens with a start,
And finds itself at home again in clay.—

  The waxen wings have melted from my strain,
And now like Icarus of old, it falls
From dizzy heights down to the world below,
To deal again in common things, and weave
A fabric less ambitious,—suited more
To the frail workman's powers; yet perchance
It may be that my lips some truths have told;
It may be that not all in vain my hand
Hath writ the thoughts of many a midnight hour,
When men and spirits mingle most, and thin
Grows the partition 'twixt the Seen and Known,
And that which everlasting darkness shrouds.
Peace to the dead! Within the Twilight Land
They wait our coming; and when life shall end,
May we that breathe upon this troublous globe
Find there the substance of the bright mirage,
Which all our years in vain we follow,—Peace.

THE DEATH OF BALDUR.

To ———.

I.

LADY, you ask a verse or two from me,
And ladies' askings are we know commands,
So I must rummage through my brain, and see
On what old lumber I can lay my hands;
Not that I wish my offering bad to be,
But that just now the stock in trade which stands
In my Pierian workshop, is not fit
To stand a fair one's overhauling it.

II.

'Tis long since Madam Muse has paid a visit
Within that somewhat dusty tenement,
And when she did come,—then ahem! I wis it
Was only to distrain for last year's rent;

She brought her rod in pickle, and to kiss it,
As Byron says, I had to be content,
So you'll perceive the reason why my rhyme
Flows not as once it flowed in olden time.

III.

Once in a pleasant sort of inspiration
I sung of sun, moon, stars and ladies' eyes,
Of all the many things that please the nation,
Of all that young men love, and greybeards prize,
Love, fame, and money, wit, rank, power, high station,
And every mortal thing below the skies,
But now my Pegasus has gone dead lame,
And I (confound it,) don't know who's to blame.

IV.

I fed the brute on oats for which I paid——
No matter what; I groomed him with a care
Worthy a Derby favourite; he repaid
My labour by objecting to the air
When for some lofty flight the start I made—
In fact, he wouldn't start for anywhere;
And so by Muse and Pegasus deserted
My verse was left to crawl in mire, and dirtied.

V.

What shall I do? a stern command is laid
On me to poetize, and yet the wings
And plumes which late I in the sun displayed
Are now become but very useless things;
The mire I lately spoke of down has weighed
My pinions, (that is, my imaginings,)
My power of song is lost, my harp is broken,
My words of passion rusty, old, unspoken.

VI.

What shall I write? 'Tis difficult to pen
Aught when the spirit moves not, and I hate
To scribble rubbish and erase again
Impatiently the words I writ so late;
Would it not be as well to wait the when
A "winged thought" shall come into my pate,
And bear my fancy, like a gas balloon,
To some far land a mile beyond the moon?

VII.

The moon, we know, is a poetic place,
Witness the many rhymes and sonnets to her;
Some men discover in her orb a face,
Some (dogs and puppies) with sweet music woo
    her;

Yet I must say I've always failed to trace
Quite as completely as in pot or ewer
Her eyes and nose, although a bard's first duty
'S to swear she's an incomparable beauty.

VIII.

Most poets live in cloudland half their days,
'Tis a verse-bearing country,—not that I
Insinuate that thence proceed my lays.
For till all lowlier Hippocrenes run dry
I'll not ascend to such a lofty place,
But rest content in meaner company,
And stick to terra firma, which I find
Is suited best to a prosaic mind.

IX.

I hate a long preamble,—I'll dispense
By your kind leave with preface, and begin;
The tale I tell shall be its own defence,
And as it merits, praise or censure win.
Then if the former be my recompense
The better luck is mine; if not, my sin
Will find me out, for critics soon arraign us,
And make each trivial blunder something heinous.

X.

So, lady, if my work is not so good
As that of many a more ambitious bard,
Judge, I beseech you, rather what I would
Than what I have writ;—if the tale be marred
'Tis not its fault but mine; and if I should
Attain to some perfection, my reward—
The best I hope,—will be that this slight strain,
If it amuse you, was not sung in vain.

THE DEATH OF BALDUR.

 WILL that ye who list to this my song
Shall pardon if an erring note go wrong,
For when men stray among the ways of old,
And sing the songs of ancient days, the gold
Full easily escapes the careless eye,
And leaves but dross behind,—the grains that lie
Among the chaff are scattered on the ground,
And nought is left but jingle of thin sound
From full deep resonance of olden lays.
   There is a fable of these ancient days
Of one that was right beautiful, and fair
Of face and favour, and of goodly air,
Such as might make a man full blithe to see,
Baldur the son of Odin and of Frea,
That were of legends of the Heathenesse.

These tales to fashion into Christian dress
I wot it is no light or easy task;
Therefore of your good patience shall I ask,
That if in any matter I transgress,
Or mar the story of mere witlessness,
Ye shall not be too quick to mark offence
Of one whose singing hath but small pretence
To aught save echo of another's harp:
For if ye be full critical and sharp
I doubt my verse may hardly this abide.
If ye be set to jape and to deride
I pray you read not of this history,
But turn the leaf thereon and let it be.

This Baldur was a god both great and wise,
That dwelt within a palace of the skies
Wherein they say king Odin holdeth feast
With many knights, of whom I trow the least
For strength were as the might of twenty men,
And tall of stature as the bulk of ten.
And these be they that in right famous wars
Have fallen after many grievous scars
Across the foemen whom their hands have slain,
And are by maidens of that fated train
That choose the souls before ordained to death
Borne to Valhalla's halls, ere yet the breath

Hath died within their nostrils;—these be they
That when blithe night-time followeth toilsome day,
The livelong hours from out the skulls of those
That in old time were of their doughtiest foes,
Drink yellow mead in halls of yellow gold,
With song and mirth and many a story told
Of deeds that were right stout and full of praise,
And merrie minstrelsie of godlike lays.
This Baldur, then, of whom my tale I tell,
How that he died and sped from heaven to hell
And dreary prison house of Hela's land,
Was of the chief of this most goodly band,
And son, as I before have tellen ye,
Of mighty Odin and his consort Frea,
That is as Venus of the Latin lore:
Who ere she bore him some short while before
Had in her fancy dremen on strange dreams,
As that she strayed beside the mighty streams
That run among the three far-stretching roots
Of that great ash-tree Ygg-Drasill, whose shoots
And leafy branches bearen up the earth,
And as she strayed had straightway given birth
Unto a filmy spirit that had wings,
Whereon a multitude of evil things
Did rise from out the water, and essay
How that they might this airy spirit slay,

But might not harm, for as they drewen nigh
This spirit spredden of its wings to fly
And so escaped, until there came a hand
That with its fingers held nor spear nor brand,
But thick green branches plucken from a tree
And touched the wings withal: then suddenly
These wings did shrivel up and all the throng
Of loathsome shapes with fierce triumphant song
Did take and drag the spirit to the waves,
Which gapen on them as do hungry graves
Upon the corpses that are set therein,
Or fiends upon some soul whose deadly sin
Hath given them power upon it for to harm.
Thereat she woke in great and dire alarm,
And when they asken of old Mimir's skull
What this might mean, its speech was dark and dull
So that they might not riddle out the rede
That lay therein, but ere I shall proceed
Now will I tell ye who this Mimir was.

In days of old the Future's misty glass
Was not involved in such obscurity
As in these latter times that now be;
And in these days there lived a seer sage
Beyond the wont of even that wise age,
Who as from writings in a book could tell
From hidden things of Nature's page, full well

The things that should in after-ages be,
Which eyes of them that were not born should see,
And hands of them that were not fashioned do.
And of his words not one thing failed of true,
But whatsoever he had prophesied
Was all fulfilled; and ere this seer died
He techen Odin great and wondrous store
Of secret mysteries and hidden lore,
And said moreover if that they should take
And hang his skull in Odin's hall, and make
A crown thereto of precious gems and gold,
That as in life it had the future told
It should not losen of this power in death,
For that the subtil wisdom of its breath
When that they willed to ask of anything
Should rest again upon its lips, and bring
True answer back to him that should inquire.
When then she dremen of this portent dire
This goddess asken what the thing should mean,
But little knowledge did she win I ween,
For that the skull made answer on this wise,
" There is that seemeth fearful to the eyes
Yet in the hand thereof doth hold no harm,
Again there is that beareth deadly charm
Wherein is nothing terrible to see;
If that ye will to counsel take of me

When ye shall have a son both brave and fair,
Then if ye will that everything shall swear
That he shall live of it withouten let,
Then shall ye nothing that is made forget,
So shall he live and prosper in his ways:
But if ye miss of one small thing, his days
Shall of that one small thing be broughten low,
That had no seeming harm therein; but know
That all my magic may no further see,
For that shall surely be which is to be."

When then that they had hearden on this wise,
Straightway there did no little question rise,
What might be hidden in this mystery,
Nor was there any of them that could see
Or fashion him to rede the rede aright;
As Daniel telleth that the hand did write
Before the eyes of that ungodly king
In midst of all his Paynim wine-bibbing
What none of all his priests might understand,
Nor was there found in that Chaldean land
One to interpret to this Belshazzar,
Save Daniel that was broughten from afar
With them that were of the captivity,
And did of all men do most righteously
Before the sight of Him that is on high.

But here I wot as well ye may espy
They lack'd of such a wise interpreter,
For that there was not any follower
Of Him that to the simple man doth give,
That doth His will and faithfully doth live,
Of His full well of knowledge to drink deep,
And showeth of His will in thoughts of sleep,
And in the visions of the silent night
Out of great darkness bringeth perfect light,
And sunshine out of much obscurity.
And here I will that ye shall pause and see
What manner of gods our fathers worshipped,
That hadden eyes implanted in their head
Yet mote not see, and ears that could not hear,
And souls that were a-dread for very fear
Of her that was their mistress, Destiny,
Nor could they turn nor alter her decree,
Nor save themselves from ill that was to come:
These be of they that having mouths are dumb,
As saith the Psalmist in his holy book,
Wherein if ye shall diligently look
Ye shall find out this Scripture that I tell,
If hitherto ye have not mark'd it well,
Or be not learned in the Latin tongue
Wherein these Psalms are every Sabbath sung,
That they may turn to your eternal weal,

Who are of Godis covenant the seal,
And first fruits of His kingdom on this earth.

  When that this goddess then had given birth
Unto a son that was right fair of face,
I trow they tarried but a little space
Ere Odin senten many messengers,
The tale whereof in this my latter verse
God wot it hardly profiteth to tell.
These messengers did traverse earth and hell,
And heaven and air and waters of the seas,
And everything that bloweth with the breeze,
And every land that lurketh underground,
Until they them had with this promise bound
That none of all the things that were therein
Should do unto this child or scathe or sin;
And all these things they asken one by one,
Yea everything that is beneath the sun
How small soever in its humbleness,
More than I could for lack of time express,
If that my lore might serven so to do,
And took of them an oath right strong and true
This Baldur should be hurten not of these.
But as they pass'd among the forest trees
There was one plant that did their search escape,
That doth with green and bushy boughen drape

The stems of treen that be full great of age,
And on their juices findeth pasturage,
And nourisheth itself of their decay.
This plant is that that in our Christian day,
When all men joy at time of Christe's birth,
Is hungen overhead with blithesome mirth,
Whereunder if shall any maiden go
He that would take a kiss of her I trow
May thus much grace himself withouten shame,
For such is custom of the merrie game;
Whereof I think ye all of you shall know
This plant I tell of is the mistletoe.
This then was bounden by no sort of oath,
For neither had it plighted of its troth,
Nor did they wot of this forgetfulnesse,
But pass'd it by in very heedlessnesse,
So that they might not turn to it again,
Whereof did issue many an after pain
As presently I shall unfold to you.
This Baldur then in lusty godhead grew,
And wroughten many deeds of deathless fame,
And made himself a great and worthy name.
As were there space I could set forth and tell,
How that he pent the giants up in hell:
In cheerless fetters of thrice-frozen ice,
And how there was not any ill device

That might avail to worken to his harm,
Because that sword and spear as by a charm
For bond of this great promise that was made
Might hurt him no more than a lathen blade
Such as the children use to play withal.
But at this time, as I the tale recall,
When he had waxen valiant and full great,
And beautiful of form, an evil fate
And terrible fell on him in this wise,—
For when his time is come, lo each man dies,
For Fate is as the flowings of the sea,
And though men greatly strive with Destiny
For all their striving shall they not prevail,
As ye shall see at ending of my tale
Which now hath but a little space to go.

   One Loki then, as I would have ye know,
That was in ancient days as now with us
Is Godis adversary Diabolus
(Which in the Grecian tongue doth signify,
That ever will he scheme and plot and lie
So that he may some witless wight beguile,
And snare his soul by violence and guile),
This Loki then, when Odin drave him out
From fair Valhalla to the gloom without,
As did the holy king the wedding guest
That came into his presence vilely drest,

Bethought himself what evil he might do
So that he mighten cause great store of woe
To them that had decreed his punishment;
And when to this his evil soul he bent,
And thought how Baldur was beloved of all,
He deemed his death might well avenge his fall.
And to this end he made a covenant
With wolves and hags and all the cursèd rant
That swarm from out the reeking womb of hell,
And with them wrought a dark ungodly spell,
Whereby they knew that this same mistletoe,
When that King Odin's messengers did go
To take the oath of every living thing,
Was overpast in this same numbering:
And thereupon, as one that doth betray
A trusting guest to them that would him slay
Laughs Judas-wise, so through that dismal crowd
There crept an evil smile, and laughter loud
And harsh as is the sound of broken bells
Brake from their lips, as doth a stream that wells
From out the murky bosom of a cave;
For well they knew the prophecy that gave
Dark warning of an humble thing o'erpast,
That shoulden work much trouble at the last.
And straight they bound them in a fearsome curse
With many a mutter'd rune and deadly verse,

That as one man they should unto this thing
Set all their minds, and dark endeavouring;
Nor should they rest at all until was slain
This Baldur, whose bright valour was their bane,
In that as I a little hence did tell
He had fast mew'd the giant brood in hell,
That were unto these hags and were-wolves kin,
And with them bounden fast in links of sin,
And by the spells that worken unto harm,
And by the might of many a midnight charm
Wrought when the raven's plume is duskiest
Beneath sad skies as dark as is his breast,
And by the works that do men's workings mar,
And by the potency of many a star
That shineth only in an evil hour
With baleful glimmer of disastrous power;
And furthermore that long they should not wait,
Lest that perchance the crooked days of fate
Should pass ere they had done this wickedness,
And good ones wherein ill were powerless
Should come, and snatch their victim from their
       hand.

Now would I have ye all to understand,
As for these gods, that little did they wot
Of boding harm or of this hellish plot,

For at this time was feast and wassail high
Through all the regions of the sunny sky;
For this same day was day of Baldur's birth,
And merry were the banquet halls with mirth,
And shouts and laughter of the goodly throng,
And singing strings of harps and harping song,
And strain of many a glad and tuneful choir,
And voice of maidens and clear voice of wire.
And as about this time did Baldur sing,
And to his song kept time with lute-playing,
For he was skilfullest singer of them all,
And well I wot did these his song recall
Through the long length of songless after-days,
And silence of the breath of stirring lays,
And silence of the lips that should no more
Wake all men's souls to echo of their lore,
And all men's hearts to echo of their fire,
Through all the hours of wearisome desire
Of dead and perish'd songs of perish'd days,
And moveless lips, and moveless hands, whose praise
That they were once melodious as the morn
Is but as wreaths that early graves adorn,
And speak of sights that shall be no more seen,
And twilight of the noonday that hath been,
And distant songs of distant youthful hours.

Is it the will of those imperious powers
Whereof we may not spy the least intent,
That soon should song and voice of song be spent,
While harsh and songless mouths eat bread, and
    live?
Is it that these harmonious spirits give
Swanlike with song their voices to the air,
And pass away like flames of breathing prayer
That utter forth their melody and die,
And with their music mount upon the sky,
And are as things whose names have pass'd away
And are as flowers of a faded day,
And dreams that death hath deluged in the sea?

Once in old time it happen'd unto me
That tell this tale to know of such an one,
And ere his singing life was well begun
Death stay'd the stream, and brake the golden bowl
And loosed the silver settings of the soul,
And tare the harping spirit's strings in twain:
Yet still a voice I may not hear again,
In musings of my head upon my bed
Rings ghostlike through the gloom when night is
    dead,
And down the dark to dawn of morning flies,
And drives the hovering slumber from mine eyes;

And in mine ears that strain upon each sound
Cries as from dismal caverns underground,
" Alas ! the sweet, sad songs of other days."

 These be the souls that journey through strange
   ways,
And with the blended flood whence Love and Sleep,
And Death and Life, and hidden things and deep
Of other worlds draw hidden founts of song,
Float down earth's streams, and as they sail along
Catch the wind's soul like wild Æolian lyres,
And turn its tones of air to kindling fires
That lap the mind in warm and genial heat,
Lend heavenward aspirations wings more fleet,
And sweetening all men's lives fall faint and die.

 Vain were it to explore this destiny,
Perchance it is not mournful as it seems,
Perchance Death's gifts are sleep and happy dreams,
Perchance this life is but the first estate—
The stern beginning of a smiling fate,
And they that soonest go find soonest rest,
And soonest cease from empty bootless quest
Of pearls that hands of clay may never find !
Perchance these see where mortal eyes are blind,
And hear where ears of men are deaf as stones ;

Perchance these sit enthroned on golden thrones,
And in that light man may not enter, stand
In long white dazzling robes at God's right hand,
And sing as never song was heard on earth ;
Perchance they but exchangen woe for mirth,
One moment's song for songs of timeless years,
That are not wet with any salt of tears,
Nor wail with any fateful undertone.

Now will I leave these later griefs alone,
And tell ye in few words how Baldur died.
When that their souls with feast were satisfied
These gods began full many a blithesome sport,
And many a mimic tourney fight was fought:
Swift feet of runners stroven for the prize
With well-braced sinews and sharp eager eyes
Set on the lessening distance of the goal,
Wherein their present thought was centred whole,
As that were all the end of lithesome strength ;
And when the race was runnen out at length,
Full sweet their rest beneath the kindly shade
Of cool thick boughs of trees, that shelter made
Where they might lie and sun them in the light
Of eyes that at their triumph grew more bright,
Or gave the barely beaten loser praise
More sweet I ween than crown of laurel bays.

Then after other fights were foughten out
From all the throng there rose one mighty shout
As Baldur all unarm'd of sword and mail
With five arm'd warriors strove and did prevail,
For that he cast them down upon the ground,
And was not hurt of any single wound
Of sword or spear, for such might harm him not.
Then 'gan he stand upon a grassy plot,
And at him cast they many a deadly thing,
And many an arrow at his breast did wing,
Which might not harm him more than feather down.
But right anon, as doth a vengeful frown
Upon the brows of some grim Eastern king,
Dark Loki crept among the merrie ring,
And in his hand a bough of mistletoe;
Then up to Baldur's brother did he go
That stood a space apart, for he was blind,
And saiden, " Hoder, blithe am I to find
That all things here above be well with ye.
Now am I come in friendship verily,
That I may make my peace with any one
To whom aforetime have I mischief done;
And if it may be, first of all would I
Pay court to Baldur yonder, whom I spy,
Standing unharm'd amid an iron hail.

Yet hardly may my wish thus much avail,
For I that as ye know was cast out hence
May barely as I think find good pretence
To join in any pastime with these knights,
Till that my former ill be set to rights,
And I myself restored, and penance done.
But as I wis this game hath well begun,
Take thou this branch that I have here with me,
And throw thou it at him, that he may see,
When thou shalt tell him whose was this device,
That Loki would find favour in his eyes,
That in the old time was his enemy
And in his sight did ill and wickedly.
For as I think I may not more express
All admiration of his nobleness,
Than that I thus should somewhat at him cast
As in the days that now are overpast;
And as in token all ill deeds should cease
Here have I brought this olive branch of peace."

Then Hoder answer'd him: "This shall be done;
And when that thou hast grace and pardon won
From Father Odin, turn not thou again
To deeds that of themselves bring fruit of pain,
For ever sorrow comes of what is ill.
Yet had I deem'd thee rather strong to kill

By force or wile, than thus to turn thy feet
From paths of guile to ways that be right meet
For one that doth repent him of his sin;
Yet if thou dost in very deed begin
From all thine evil works to turn away,
Now will I give thee whatso help I may.
And first will I this branch at Baldur cast,
And when this noise of mirth be somewhat past
Then will I tell him of thy good intent;
And doubt not mine endeavour shall be bent
As well as in me lieth to thy weal,
To binden fast all broken faith, and heal
These breaches that thy sometime deeds have made,
And stablish peace that hath been long delay'd."
Then as he spake he took this mistletoe;
But when that he did it at Baldur throw
Soon as it touch'd him straightway fell he dead,
As lilies fall that droopen low their head,
And bow beneath the blast that breaks the stem.

This then was end of Loki's stratagem,
And now with end thereof my tale is told.
And as a traveller, that doth behold
His journey's close, half joyous and half sad,
So look I on this verse that I have clad
In many-colour'd robes of Poesie,

And gaze thereon, and leave full lothfully.
Yet must each thing that hath beginning end,
And from its birth toward its closing wend,
Even as this tale: yet if ye thinken well,
I may again some further story tell
Of these same fables of the olden days.

   Now let us give to God all thank and praise,
So shall He bless the labour of our hands,
And pour out peace and plenty through these lands
And keep our souls from Satan and from hell,
Until we see His face in heaven.
Farewell.

WITCH-SONG ON THE DEATH OF BALDUR.

GLOOMILY wave the sepulchral trees
    Over thine early grave;
The owl hoots long her mournful song
    O'er one whom nought can save;
While the desolate bank with its reedbeds rank
    The stream of the dead doth lave.

The stream of the dead in its doleful bed
    Flows on with a moaning sound,
While troops of the silent and shivering shades
    Throng ghostly all around:
All travel along the same dark road,
    To the same black haven bound.

And thou with them shalt travel soon,
    Head of the mournful throng,

By the light of the pale and ghastly moon
    Hurrying swiftly along;
Lo thou canst see the spectres dim,
    And hear their funeral song.

We see thee, we see thee, thou travell'st apace
    The road whence none return,
Thou mayst not depart from the fated race
    Though thy heart within thee burn,
Though thy soul consume, and thou tremble with
        fear
    Like a hart in the cold rank fern.

Thy soul is the prey of the souls that devour,
    So lay thee down and die,
We longingly wait for thy last faint hour,
    And the glance of thy glazing eye.
Oh! merrily, merrily, shall we dance
    When thou in the tomb dost lie!

We have done, we have done, and the spell is
        begun,
    Oh! glad is the Weaver of Harm,
In the pine wood he drinketh the warm blood of
        men,
    The mighty, hag-born, Managarm:

And the witch-wives scream with a yell of joy
    At the strength of their own dark charm.

Ay, strong is the spell, and it worketh well,
    Nought may avail to save;
Soon in dark Hela's fearful halls
    Thou shalt list to the sough of the wave,
Like a fierce and sullen beast of prey,
    In some black mountain cave.

Gloomily wave the sepulchral trees
    Over thine early tomb,
And they rustle and moan in the desolate breeze,
    Lamenting thy terrible doom;
For soon hast thou sped from the dawn of thy morn
    To the midnight of sorrow and gloom.

Oh! strong is the charm of the Weaver of Harm,
    And the omen of coming sorrow,
Play, play, like the doomed lamb to-day,
    Thou shalt be with the dead to-morrow!
So in and out let us dance about,
    While the forms of wolves we borrow.

The were-wolves sing in the charmed ring
    With many a rune and spell,

Mayst hear them chanting their deadly rhyme
    Like the boom of some distant bell;
And the gibber of scorn keeps time, keeps chime,
    With the pulse of the nethermost hell!

Gloomily wave the sepulchral trees
    To the notes of the owlet's cry,
The vulture flies through the leaden skies,
    Which frown as he hurries by,
Wail, wail, ye hated deities,
    For Baldur's doom is nigh!

'Tis nigh,—but how 'twill come none knows
    Save the hags whom all despise;
'Tis mournful and dark as the cypress boughs,
    When the bat among them flies:
'Tis like the sound of a coming storm,
    Or ever the winds arise.

Full darkly o'er its slimy shore,
    With many a dreary groan,
The stream of the dead flows on for aye,
    While the reeds around it moan;
And thy soul shall wander among the reeds,
    Desolate and alone.

So in, and out, and round about,
    Let's dance in fearful glee,
For through the expanse of the widespread world
    Who so wise as we?
And the death of the young, the fair, the good,
    Is a glorious sight to see!

A LAY OF THE LIFE OF MAN.

I.

ONE afternoon I wander'd forth in dreams,
   And found a forest full of fairy flowers,
And sweet with warbling notes of many streams,
   And wealth of many strange, fantastic bowers;
And through the leaves there roamed a voice that cried,
     "Oh! follow, follow,"
And bee-like fled among the forest wide,
     From hill to mossy hollow:
And as my steps thereafter stray'd, I spied
   Twain women clad from head to foot in white,
   And twain that wore long raiment dark as night,
And songs of these smote all the air, and died.

II.

The first of them was large and lithe like Spring,
    And in her hands she held a silvern harp;
Her breast was full of flowers blossoming,
    And through her hair strange colour-play struck
        sharp,
As moonbeams strike long levels of the sea:
        Her limbs were round and white,
    And all her cheeks like down of peach-blossom,
        Her eyes as dewdrops bright
That nestle in the snowy vale-lily;
    Her breath was like bruised frankincense, and
        gum
    Of dragon trees, and scented galbanum,—
And all her body one long harmony.

III.

The next was like the breath of yellow flame
    Fleck'd red with heaviness of ripen'd fruit:
Her eyes were as the eyes of birds half tame,
    And on her lips wild gusts of sighs sank mute:
And on her breasts there glow'd a subtle fire;
        And round about her knees
Her robe flow'd down, and left her bosom bare
        As sunny naked seas.

And in her hands she held a breathing lyre
    Wreathed round with myrtle and red berries fair,
    Within the breast whereof each wandering air
Swept lovelike, kissing sound from every wire.

IV.

The third was like the braided hair of night:
    Her brows were with dark ivy garlanded,
And in her cheeks no warm blood dyed the white,
    And in her lips was wealth of music dead,
That might not rouse itself to any sound
        Save songs of slumbering hours.
    Her arms were full of dusky poppy sheaves,
        Thick yew, and hemlock flowers,
That from her hands fell loosely to the ground:
    Her robe was black, with long star-spangled sleeves;
    Her smile was as the latter autumn leaves,
Her face like thought that in the deep is drown'd.

V.

The last was like the bow'd and blighted corn
    Whose ears are grey as with exceeding age,
Or as the night that recks not of the morn,
    Or nodding plumes of funeral equipage.
And in her hand she held a barbed spear,

And sad and sterile grain
Was wreathed about her brows of heavy snow,
That lower'd, yet smiled through pain.
And in each eye there stood one full round tear,
And her lips quiver'd into speech as low
As is the speech of sleepy streams, that flow,
And, as they float and murmur, muse of fear.

VI.

Then as my feet drew nigh, the first one smiled,
Shook back long locks of silk and sunny gold,
And sang a strain as warm and wonder-wild
As is the summer sun that kills the cold.
And as she sang my soul spread forth its wings
As doth the lark at morn,
And as her fingers danced among the strings
Soar'd forth new born;
And woke to sights of many secret things,
And little sounds of life below the earth,
Dim mystic melodies of shapeless birth,
And paths of distant fearless wanderings.

VII.

And I became a little child again,
And there was one that took me by the hand,

And led me to a flush'd and panting plain
   Of wild empurpled western colour-land:
And on the clouds I saw fleet shapes with wings,
        That from the crimson haze
   Grew into form, and faded fast again,
           And fled through footless ways.
And I was as a bird that soars and sings
   Till ecstasy of spirit sinks to pain,
   And all my thoughts became as pearls of rain,
And dreams of many-hued imaginings.

VIII.

My guide was as a young and lovely bride,
   That with late morning from the bride-chamber
Comes blushing forth, and still unsatisfied
   Thinks on past joy that yet entrances her:
And as she caught me up into her arms
        I straight became a man.
   And of the four the first one ceased her play;
        The second one began.
And all my heart was fill'd with soft alarms,
   I turn'd me to my love, and down the day
   My soul was lost within her locks astray
Like gold on snow, and nestled in her arms.

IX.

And all my limbs wax'd warm with ripening heat,
    And great life burnt and trembled through my veins,
And to my lips her lips became as meat,
    Her eyes like wine, her wandering hands as chains,
Soft silken chains, as light as spider's thread.
        But as I turn'd and sigh'd
    The second singer hush'd her fiery strain,
        And all the vision died.
And there was one that came to me, and said,
    "Love's thread is broken from thy being's skein,
Lo, here I come, Love's elder sister, Pain,
And tell thee that thy goodly days are dead."

X.

And as she spake my heart became a stone,
    And Hope became a sad unmeaning word,
And Joy a flower that with the morn is mown,
    Love a told tale, and Fame a voice unheard.
And nought I felt but deadness of desire,
        And weary weight of woe,
    And there was nothing that seem'd bright or fair

In all the earth below.
My breast was as the brand of a dead pyre,
  My lips as dry as gusts of desert air,
  The palace of my soul a dismal lair
Of owls and bats, and wasting worm of fire.

XI.

Then from the lips of the third singer came
  A whisper as of waters murmuring,
That dewlike fell upon the arid flame
  Of my dry life, as rain at evening
Falls upon thirsty leaves of drooping flowers;
    And slumber came to me,
  And in and out among my limbs did go,
    In low monotony
Of sleepy songs of heavy scented bowers,
  And wings of night that waver to and fro,
  And airs that lull the loneliness of woe,
And sighing strains of slumberous spirit showers.

XII.

And ever as she sang she smiled on me,
  And pity sank and trembled in her eyes,
As midnight stars that glimmer in the sea,
  Or flame that in its own faint fervour dies.
And thus her music ran, " Sleep, wanderer, sleep,

And woes shall waste away;
Forget the love that lost is turn'd to bane,—
The clouds that dim thy day.
Rest, and let drowsy dews thy spirit steep,
I may not give thee back thy dreams again,
Yet may I scare away the steps of Pain,
And drown sick longing deeper than the deep."

XIII.

And long I slept and had sweet rest from sorrow,
And long she sang as summer night-winds sing:
Alas! each morning melts upon to-morrow,
Summer to autumn, winter-time to spring.
And when she ceased my grief came back again,
And wearier than before;
Then as I turn'd to her she sigh'd, and said,
"No more, no more!"
And I beheld and close at hand was Pain;
I closed mine eyes, but lo, my sleep was dead,
Sharp thorns were girdled round about my head,
My cheeks were sad as rivers red with rain.

XIV.

Then I arose and wail'd, and call'd on Death,
And straight the last dark singer woke to song,

And came to me and kiss'd away my breath,
    And said, " Mine own, thy rest is deep and long,
Nor shall Pain vex thy spirit any more ;
        My lips have press'd thy brow,
    Is not my kiss more sweet than honey streams
        To souls that break and bow ?"
Then my wild heart was silenced to the core,
    My soul awoke, or sank in dreams of dreams,
    Fled with the clouds, and shone in starry beams,
Saw wond'rous sights, and learnt strange secret
    lore.

XV.

Then said I, " Life is woe and weariness,
    Though all her face wax fervent as the sun,
And Death is rest and wordless happiness,
    And welcome sound of thankless labour done ! "
For all my soul was light as curling smoke,
        And on the streams and flowers
    Cast all its essence, and among the trees
        Spread itself out in showers;
Or wavelike on the rocks of being broke,
    And sported on the gladness of the seas,
    Or lovelike hung on every passing breeze,
And kiss'd each flower till all its sweetness
    woke.

XVI.

These be the four that sing to every man,
    Strong Life, fierce Passion, Sleep, and kindly Death,
And as their strain is so is each one's span,
    The chequer'd path that each man followeth.
And Life is bright, and Passion hot like wine,
    And Sleep is grave and still,
    These three pour out for man the drink of tears,
    And hungry hopes that kill;—
These build his dwelling-place of rain and shine,
    These feed his sated soul with joys and fears,—
    A little rest in many weary years:—
And all are fair, but Death is most divine.

SONG OF SLEEP.

I.

N valleys low, where shadiest reed-beds blow,
    Along the banks of stillest, laziest stream,
Where poppies glow, and sluggish waters flow,
    As flows upon the mind some drowsy dream
    A-doze or in sleep-vigil, till it seem
A very blank, where no faint thought may dwell,
    Yea in vast silence, as far planet's beam
From plain of grey dim Milky Way doth well,
My presence broods, my song breathes heavily its spell.

II.

Where meteors play along the star-paved way,
    Full of sweet tone too deep for any sound,

My music swells, and tells of vanish'd day,
    And daytime cares in balmy vintage drown'd.
    And round my head are leaves of ivy bound,
And sprigs of cypress, not of grief but rest,
    With my dark hair are in dark wreaths enwound ;
Mine arms are soft to form with toil oppress'd,
And weary brows relax upon my peaceful breast.

III.

I reign alone upon a noiseless throne,
    My black robe rustles not to any wind,
Within my realms no sound of sigh or moan
    Rises from anguish of thought-tortured mind ;
    Therein doth wearying labour respite find,
There is no seed of Sorrow's thorny weed,
    With restless Hope in mingled garland twined,
There is no need of spirit-wearing speed,
Or haste of aught, for thought is rest and rest is
    deed.

IV.

The magic of my song is wild and strong,
    Like beaded draught of potent oily wine,
And wine-like stills the quick tumultuous throng
    Of Care's unquiet hosts that war with mine ;

And cloud-like veils the blinding beams that
    shine
Full in men's eyes from glare of worldly skies,
    Blotting with dead white blaze the horizon's line
Ere rises up the night and daylight flies,
And with the day the gay distracting flame-play
    dies.

V.

Thick droops my hair upon my bosom bare,
    In twilight braided indistinctness falling,—
Through gloom wan light, that answereth voice
    of night,
    Deathlike from Slumber's starriest empire
        calling:
In speech of restful loveliness enthralling
Sad thought-sick brain, and heart whose beat is
    pain,
    And mind whose air-built phantasies appalling
Rise demon-like from wintry watery main
Of storm-vext life as mists rise from some marshy
    plain.

VI.

I steep the lids of him that lies asleep
    In heedless trance, that neither cares nor hears

How baffled Grief in vain doth wail and weep,
    That now she cannot drown his eyes in tears,
    Nor load his soul with burden of cold fears,
For nectar red of wavy poppy bed,
    That 'twixt her prey and ravening clutch uprears
A low moss bank with earthy odours spread,
A cradle soft and safe for aching feverous head.

VII.

My song is softest singing ever heard:
    For though Love's strain is warm as clasping fire,
Though Death chant clear as note of skilfullest bird,
    Yet doubt and dread and pain and dead desire,
    And many a ruin'd voice and mournful lyre,
Wake with Love's harp through Memory's mouldering cave;
    And clang of brass with mellow silvery wire,
Together vibrate in sonorous wave
When Death with iron throat takes up the closing stave.

VIII.

But welcome is my music to the ear
    Of earth and sea and everything therein,

Men lay them on my bosom free of fear
    That there shall reach them any grievous din
    Of troublous waking images, that spin
With tangled warp and woof of clamorous noise
    The pauseless web that doth with day begin
Of shadowy fears, marr'd schemes, and faded joys,
That steal man's youth away and leave no coun-
    terpoise.

IX.

Where scent of flowers hangs heaviest on the breeze
    That bows the grass on slope of greenest hill,
Save for the listless murmur of the trees
    As is the twilight or the dawning, still ;
    Where in the universal hush, the rill
Its warbling changeth to low dreamy song,
    In ear of bees that with thick honey fill
Their laden pouches as they glide along
From bloom to bloom, I smile and guide the
    whispering throng.

X.

Alike in morn and night, in dark and light,
    I am the one thing most beloved of man,
Lady of sleep which is as is delight,
    Lady of rest and drowsy airs that fan,

And draughts that soothe and lengthen life's
    brief span,
Which frosty Trouble as a rose would blight,
    And envious Anguish, ever watchful, ban,
And wolfish Discontent like hunger bite,
And gnaw the spirit's soul ere the soul's self take
    flight.

XI.

Then come ye to mine arms all ye that mourn,
    And ye shall rest you from your heaviness,
Afar from pain, afar from scathing scorn,
    Afar from every thought of weariness:
    And peace shall be the broidery of your dress,
And sleep shall be upon you like a veil,
    And Love shall tarry near at hand to bless,
And woe shall be but as a weary tale,
And grief a thing that was, and pain a phantom
    pale.

XII.

Love, life, and morn give joy, but I give rest,
    And pity deeper than the depths of sea,
And songs from fairy islands of the West;
    Then all ye weary wanderers come to me,

And dreamless shall your placid slumber be,
And lightly shall ye rise and go your ways,
   Fill'd full of might that bids all faintness flee,
And sleep that fits the frame for toilsome days,
And strengthens sinking souls to sing my silent praise.

THREE YEARS AGO.

A MODERN IDYLL.

THREE years ago! yet one it scarcely seems,
Time is so intermix'd with thoughts and dreams,
Since this now wither'd flower was given to me;
Then it was green and fresh and fair to see,
As were the hopes that with those hours were fed,
And now like them its life and bloom are fled.
Methinks I see again that April day,
So glad, so warm, all nature seem'd at play,
When through the upland lanes two young men rode
To where among the trees and hills abode
She whose hand pluck'd this flower to give to me.
Our hearts were light, and we rode merrily,

Though soon for years we were to part, for he
Was in some months to sail across the sea,
In distant lands to seek for wealth; while I,
Bound down to home by many a subtle tie,
Cared not 'neath other skies and stars to roam,
But as a poor physician kept at home;
Though spite of work I found some time to play,
And now enjoy'd fresh air and holiday
Within my father's quiet country seat,
Where all was joying in the spring-time sweet.

Slowly we rode, in the warm April breeze,
Until a house appear'd among the trees,
In at whose gate we turn'd, and at the door
We met the eldest of the sisters four
Who with their mother and their brother there
Lived 'mong the mountains and the woodlands fair.
And in we pass'd, and sat and talk'd awhile
Some minutes few ere luncheon to beguile;
Then in the youngest sister came, and she
Shook hands with both, and came and sat by me,
And talk'd in low sweet accents, asked me how
I fared, said she was glad to see me now,
Though somewhat late in calling: and I spoke
As one that from a sleep is just awoke,
And still half dreams—for Love can never speak

One half his hoarded secret; but my cheek
Although not used to blush was flush'd with red,
And to this day I know not what I said.
Most like 'twas foolish;—how it is man proves
An idiot only to the girl he loves,
When to all others he can talk at will,
I know not: but it pass'd my utmost skill
Then to converse on aught; she laugh'd may be
At my poor powers of talking, and at me,
Yet was she kind, half loving, and in brief,
The great bell rang and luncheon brought relief.
And when 'twas o'er we in the garden stray'd,
Saw the new greenhouse that had just been made,
In which she pluck'd this flower and gave it me;
And I have kept it ever since, while she
Forgets perchance both it and me together:
But this I know, through calm and stormy weather,
Whate'er befall, I ne'er shall lose the flower,
Nor the remembrance of that blissful hour,
Though all the bliss was but fool's Paradise,
A glamour and a mockery of the eyes.
And then we wander'd out upon the moor,
Her sister and my comrade on before,—
We two behind: and presently we came
To where a noisy, rushing, mountain stream
Flow'd down a glen, with banks on either side

Thick-wooded, and across the torrent wide
A bridge of stone, and on the other bank
Half hid by foliage of the branches rank
A tower, such as on the banks of Rhine
Is many a one; but this as I divine
Was but a house when nearer seen, and stood
On the glen-top above the tract of wood,
And standing thus appeared much magnified,
When from a distance seen. Then by the side
Of the swift stream, upon a rustic seat
We sat, nor noted how the moments fleet
Sped as we talk'd, for then my thoughts came back,
And my words too: yet did I courage lack
To tell her all was in my mind, and how
I loved her,—and I cannot tell her now!
I should have spoken then; 'tis now too late—
I seldom see her in these days, and Fate
Seems to have built a barrier twixt us twain,
That were so near each other, which again
To cross were as recrossing desert lands,
Without a compass, upon unknown strands.

Then we arose, and our way homeward made,
Yet for some moments on the bridge we stay'd,
And look'd into the water, and her face
Shone in the water with a double grace.

Oh! she was very beautiful to see,
As my heart knew, and knows, alas! for me.
I never can forget her, though my days
And paths have led me over many ways
Where the world walks, and where fair women
      be,—
Fairer perchance: yet did I never see
One whose least look could set my soul on fire
As hers could; one within whose hair Desire
Sat like a queen, enthroned in burnish'd gold,
And caught my heart, as Lilith's hair of old
Wound like a net around men till they died.
She was my love, my angel, and my pride:
It may be that I painted her more bright
Because I loved her; that my partial sight
Saw not the errors other eyes would see,
For very blaze of light that dazzled me:—
All this may be, but yet my love returns,
Though oft half quench'd, and ever fiercer burns.

  As we came back again the church-bell's chime
Rang out the hour of four, and now 'twas time
To bring our pleasant visit to an end,
For we had some eight good long miles to wend
Back to my father's, where that day we dined;
And so we left, and still I thought how kind

And gentle was her manner as we parted.
Could it be she too was not quite whole hearted?
I never knew: and yet she press'd my hand,
As though it were to make me understand
I was not all unwelcome,—that one heart
Would beat a little for my sake, apart
From friendship merely ; yet next time we met
Her looks were cold, her phrases short and set,
And so I never told her she was dear
To me beyond all other things that were,
And now shall never tell her while I live,
Though life I think has little more to give
Save dull content, and gold perchance, and fame,
The dreary blossom of a barren name.
—My brain is weary, and I fain would rest
Upon some lovely sympathizing breast ;
And yet perforce must face the world alone,
Advise and cure the while I inly groan,
More deeply sick than those I hourly heal.
Would that the mind could case itself in steel,
And shut remembrance out!—it may not be,
Oblivion comes but with Eternity.

THE WHITE BIRD.

A BALLAD.

I.

SIR Otto paced adown his hall
    One stormy winter night,
The ruddy fire-glow on the wall
    Shone out full warm and bright,
And drear outside the night-wind sigh'd,
    And flash'd the lightnings' light.

II.

Beside the fire old Peter sits
    Warming his ancient frame;
An hundred years have left his wits
    Wiser than ere they came,
And learning great is in his pate,
    Though old and deaf and lame.

III.

He poreth o'er an ancient tome,
    And reads and sits and sighs,
Then looketh forth into the night
    With sad half-curious eyes,
And opens wide the lattice side,
    When in a white bird flies.

IV.

A snow-white bird with golden beak,
    Ne such was ever seen,
Its feathers wet, its pinions weak,
    The delicate sea green
That was its eye was bright and dry,
    Full fair to see I ween.

V.

About the hall the white bird flies,
    Sir Otto stops his walk,
Without the wild wind howls and sighs,
    Within is mirth and talk;
Nor doth there fail of good brown ale,
    And work for knife and fork.

VI.

It resteth on the mantelshelf
    Above old Peter's head,

Of all was good they brought it food,
    Yet would it not be fed;
But wink'd its eye so bright and dry,
    And to the lattice sped.

VII.

Out, out into the howling night
    They watch'd it wildly fly,
As if it were some goblin sprite,
    Nor could they further spy—
They saw the white blend with the night,
    And vanish from the eye.

VIII.

"What means this chance?" Sir Otto cried
    With face as pale as stone,
Henchman and page were stupefied,
    Old Peter calm alone;
"Methinks," quoth he, "that I can see
    This matter to the bone.

IX.

"Man's soul comes out of darkness first
    Unto this weary earth,
And there doth stray, a toilsome way
    Unto its death from birth,

Then into darkness goes again,
    And leaves both pain and mirth.

X.

"This white bird clean that we have seen,
    He is as is man's soul,
Into the light so warm and bright,
    From darkness black as coal,
He comes, awhile rests in its smile,
    Then flieth to his goal.

XI.

"And though to all, both great and small,
    The grave is dark and deep,
Yet live thou well, and men shall tell
    Thy virtues as they weep;
The silent tear upon thy bier
    Shall soothe thee in thy sleep."

XII.

Old Peter walk'd from out the hall,
    To each man bade adieu,
A quiet grace was on his face
    For he the warning knew.—
Men laid their heads upon their beds,
    And night to morning flew.

XIII.

The morning came with sunny flame,
    And lit the skies with red,
Sir Otto and his men arose,
    And steed and hound were fed;
But Peter old, as it is told,
    Was found that daybreak dead.

THE LONELINESS OF POWER.

> ——" Alone, why so should be
> Creators and destroyers."
> *Death's Jest Book.* BEDDOES.

LONE, all all alone,
    Alone in the heart of the teeming town,
    Alone in the tumbling tide of men,
Jostling, elbowing, up and down,
Swaying, tossing, to and fro,
Ebbing, flowing, ebbing again,
Rising, sinking, high and low,
All alone like a ghost that flits
Back to its earthly home,
Alone as a bird that sits
On a ruin'd roof in a desolate land,
Where man has forgot to roam,
Where the sky has forgotten his face,
And the ground forgotten his feet,

And the land forgotten his hand,
And the wind forgotten his dwelling place,
And the sand his tread on the sand.
Alone, as a swallow fleet,
Or an owl in a city of old,
That makes its nest in the fresco'd walls
That once were fretted with gold.—
Yet the owl to his fellow calls,
And the swallow flies to her mate,
But I am alone like a lonely star
Dogged by a desolate fate,
That shines in the skies afar
From the circle of other spheres,
Shining alone, early and late,
Down the dream of the years,
Glimmering down the clouds that frown
Like the haunting faces of fears.

All alone by day,
Lonelier far by night,
I sit and watch the shadow-play
Steal over the face of the sun,
I watch the clouds in the dawn of light,
And the light when the day is done.
I walk in the crowded street,
Amid the rush and the foam

THE LONELINESS OF POWER.

Of the clashing human streams that meet
Whirling away to work or to play,
These to the heart of the waves that beat
To the tide of money and fame ;
These to their quiet home
As on wearied wings of a dove,
These to the world's mad game,
These to the laughter of love.
Is there never a hand to clasp,
Is there never a breast to beat,
Is there never a voice and a kindly grasp,
An ear to listen and long
For the nearing sound of my feet,
For the heart that harps and grieves,
For the voice that fashions the song?
Is there none to join the fate
Of the weary souls that create,
Of those that weep and weave,
And sow that others may sheave,
And build that others may dwell therein,
Whose labour profits them not,
Whose prayer is turn'd to a sin,
And their raiment turn'd to a blot?

Is it that they that are great,
Whose souls are as souls of the fire

Are cursed with a sad and lonely fate
Because their visions are higher,
Because they are nearer heaven,
Because they think not as men,
And are as a working leaven,
A savour that soon or late
Shall rise and be known as sweet,
A light in a darksome den,
A grain of fruitful wheat,
That shall yield tenfold in hereafter days,—
Because their feet are as feet
Of him that sings in his ways?

One thing only I know
That is sorrow and pain to me,
That never a wind of the winds that blow
On the tempest-troubled sea,
Shall waft by night or day
Another sail the way
Where my bark sails alone,
Shall set me down in the common world
From the peak of an icy throne,
With snow-wreaths round it curl'd,
Whither some unknown power
Hath borne me not for my good,
To a crag where tempests lower,

To the depths of a mazy wood,
Far from the warmth of love,
Or fellowship of mankind,
Up to a region above,
Whence is no turning again,
No way to the lowland bowers,
No roof for shelter from showers,
No path through the quaking fen,
No balm for the troubled mind,
No light for the eyes that are blind
With the glaring beams of the sun,
No rest though the search be done,
For Peace which none can find.

Where is the wave of the wind that sweeps from
  the pinions of Passion?
Where is the breath of the blast blown from the
  bosom of Love?
Even in the valleys of earth, and with them that
  are earthly of fashion,
Sorrow not sympathy steeps souls that are
  moulded above.
  To these men knowledge is dower,
  Strength and the wisdom of power,
  These of all things that have birth
  Are born to be lonely on earth;

Those that create and destroy,
Those that cause sorrow or joy,
Those that are angel or devil,
These shall rejoice in the triumph of good or the
    triumph of evil;
These shall seek others as they,
Seek and not find,
These have their separate way,
These shall go on to their end,
Finding nor lover nor friend,
Till the snows of the winter shall close on the
    rose and the morn of their May.

And am I then of these? I know
Again another thing,
Those birds that fly not oft below
Have longer wing.
The phœnix lives on rocks and crags
A solitary life,
And though his full flight never flags,
He hath no wife.
Alone the highest mountains tower
And freeze in barren snows,
While valleys glow with many a flower
Of myrtle and of rose;

And if the lot of these be mine,
Shall not I share in shower and shine?

The dreary, rugged strength that stands
Alone in its lonely might,
Like a tower piled by giant hands,
Or the sun in his shareless robe of light,
Is a waste and weary thing,
Yet these be the lips that sing,
These be the hands that fight;
And though the face of the night be dark,
Yet knowledge comes in the night;
And though the eyes see never a spark,
The soul is clear and bright.
Then will I suffer in silence, and fall not to weeping and wailing,
Tears and tempest of sighs are weak and their rage unavailing,
There is more strength in one beam of the sun than in numberless showers,
Then will I shine if I may as I stray through the paths of the hours.

LINES SUGGESTED BY A PICTURE.

"Hope deferred maketh the heart sick."

 AM away from the sole one that loves me, from all that is dearest,
Earth is a blank, and as void as the meaningless heaven that smileth,
Cloudless and dim overhead, in the glancing light of the sunbeams,
While the monotonous round of the day journeys slowly to evening,
Slowly and slowly, as ripples the brook in the heart of the forest,
Calmly, as pass the thoughts in the mind of some loveless maiden.
Still I am thinking and dreaming awhile in the afternoon brightness,

Thinking of sights I have seen, and of memories
   dear to my mind,
Looking, and longing, and waiting in patience the
   time when the present,
Loaded with mists of the night, shall vanish away
   into morning.
Oh! I have loved and am loved, and yet I am
   tired and weary,
Weary of watching and waiting so long for the
   time that is coming,
Weary of summer and winter, and weary of birds
   and of flowers,
Weary of all the delights that once I so loved and
   rejoiced in.
Ah! what is life without love? what is love
   without happiness rather?
Merely a yearning towards the unknown, the
   unfathom'd, the endless,
Merely a sorrow, a pain, a thorn in the joy of
   existence,
Merely a gleam of light, shining out in an ocean
   of darkness.
Oh, I have waited so long and so patiently,—when
   will the end come!
When shall my sun burst forth through the clouds
   that at present obscure him?

When shall I happily love, or cease to love for
    ever?
Would I were lying asleep in the mouldering calm
    of the churchyard,
Careless of all that is done, of all that is suffer'd
    above me,
Untormented by thoughts of the past, and by fears
    for the future,
Slumbering still as a child in the clasping arms of
    its mother,
Wrapt in eternal peace, far away from earth's toils
    and its troubles.
When will he come, oh! when? I am sick, I am
    tired of living,
Oh! so weary, so weary, of waiting, and longing,
    and dreaming,
Watching the days go by, and the night close in
    on the daylight,
Watching the dark night wane in the cold grey
    morning's arising,
Watching the sparrows cling to the eaves in the
    warmth of the spring-time,
Watching the winter's snows envelop the landscape
    around me,
Watching the desolate rain run down from the old
    blacken'd windows,

Watching the leaves peep forth in the spring, and
    fall in the autumn.
'Tis but a year since we parted, and yet it seems
    like a thousand,
A vast and measureless waste, a blank in the span
    of existence,
A terrible waking dream, whose very nothingness
    frights me,
A desert of blinding space, stretching far away
    into silence.

I have heard that death is rest, and that life is but
    labour and sorrow,
One I know to be true, oh! would that the other
    were also;
For then would I lay me down, and breathe forth
    my life in the sunset,
Here as I sit on the grass, with the trees stirring
    softly above me,
Whispering in the breeze that plays through their
    leaf-laden branches,
Sighing as if in response to my sighs and tears of
    anguish.
Yet will I wait, for it may be that sooner or later
    is coming

Gladness in place of gloom, and light instead of darkness.
God thou art merciful,—try not Thy creatures beyond their endurance!
Loving and gracious art Thou, oh! look on my love then with favour,
Or, if Thou willest it so, let me die, and find rest from my troubles.

LA BELLE DAME SANS MERCI.

FAIR as the snow-white bloom on the face of a passionless lily,
Lovely as breezes that blow from the odorous lands of the West,
Sweet as the calm upon midnight seas when the heaven is stilly
Shineth the light of thy limbs, and the bloom of thy delicate breast:
Shineth in motion and tune to the throb of the pulses of Love,
As out of the midnight arises a star on an ocean of grey,
Glitters as numberless lustrous rainbows on wings of a dove,
Flashes and gleams as a lake in the maze of the sunbeams' play,
When the red sinks low in the west, at the close and the change of the day.

Yes fair, ah! fair art thou,
As Life or Sleep or Death,
And sweet as dewlit roses' breath
In summer's sunniest hours,
And sad at times as bough
Of cypress bending low,
Along a garden bed,
Among a wealth of flowers.
And round about thy head
Love weaves a crown,
Worthy a queenly brow,
Of snows, and gold, and red,
And regal blush, and brown.
And round about thy heart
Where no pain lies,—
Another's nor thine own—
There freezes too a realm of snows,
Which whoso reaches dies;
And finds his love alone,
Since echo there
Is none for all his woes,
And all his care.
And life must run to closing,
And toiling to reposing,
And waking dreams to dozing,
And Love though Love be fair.

Thy face is as a vision of the night,
  When stars break forth on stars in heaven's vast
    way,
Thy hair as threads of interwoven light,
  Thy voice as sound of mystic fairy lay.
Thy love as light as marsh fire's flickering flame,
  Upon some lonely waste;
Thy feelings but the shadow of a name,
  To him that thirsts as streams of brackish taste.

And yet we love thee; better love the form
  Pygmalion carved of marble in old time.
Man can but die, and why should wind and storm
  With life's chords in discordant response chime?
For thou art wild as wintry weather,
  And she the marble cold and still,
Why should poor mortals hand in hand together
  Meet passing beauty, blended with all ill?

Rest! we shall rest it may be in the grave,
  Yet till Death cometh we must wake and weep;
On mortal shores there is no drowsy cave,
  No draught of that cold chalice which is Sleep.
And thou art as a wind on glassy seas,
  As hurricanes upon a sunlit shore,
Who seeth thee hath done for aye with ease,
  And he that smiling meets thee smiles no more.

Ah! lovely heartless Syren of the waves,
　O'er which Ulysses-like through life we roam,
The shore about thee lieth thick with graves,
　With tears thy robes are wet instead of foam;
When wilt thou cease to make thine eyes as fire
　To burn and kill?
With wails of misery rising high and higher
　When will thy fierce soul fill?

Never methinks; yet as strain of the Muse-born
　　rang clearer than thunder,
　Rang in the hearts of the heroes that journey'd
　　with Jason of old,
Drowning the voice of the Syrens, that howl'd in
　　a passion of wonder,
　Till they leapt from the rock to the sea, and were
　　changed into stones grey and cold;
So through my frame thrills the passion of song,
　　and my soul is deliver'd,
　Yea as a bird from the snare of the fowler
　　escaped I am free;
I have torn from my bosom thine image that
　　arrow-like rankled and quiver'd,
　I am loose from the chains of my bondage,
　　and free from my thraldom and thee.

ARIADNE RELICTA.

FROM CATULLUS.

HOM[1] with sad wistful gaze from the lone shore
Like stone-carved Mœnad Ariadne sees;
She sees alas! and on the mighty waves
Of Care is toss'd, nor on her golden locks
Does she retain her finely woven head-dress,
Nor is her waist with filmy girdle bound,
Nor are her swelling breasts with gauzy robes
Confined; for at her feet the salt sea-waves
Toss these unheeded to and fro,—for she
Recks naught of head-dress nor of flowing robe:
But, Theseus, all her thoughts are fix'd on thee,
In thee is centred all her anxious care.
Ah! miserable maiden, in whose breast
Queen Erycina with unsparing hand

---

[1] Theseus.

Has sown more thorns than roses, from that time
When Theseus leaving the recurvèd shores
Of Athens and Piræus reach'd at length
The palace of the unjust Gortynian king.

   Him then the royal maid beheld, whose youth
Within her mother's soft embrace, a couch
Breathing forth odours sweet had gently reared,
As grow the myrtles on Eurotas' banks,
Or as the varied colours of the spring
Peep forth beneath the breath of gentle wind:
And as she turn'd on him her love-lit eyes,
The subtle flame seized on her inmost heart,
And quenchless burnt the marrow in her bones.
Alas! thou boy that minglest human joy
And grief together in a troubled whole,
And thou that reignest o'er the Golgi,—queen
Of the leaf-bower'd Idalia, in what waves,
What stormy waves of pain have ye engulf'd
That wretched maiden, for the yellow locks
Of her brave guest oft sighing! ah! what fears
Bore she within her fluttering heart,—how oft
Paler she grew than hue of palest gold,
When Theseus longing with the savage beast
To fight, sought death or victory's reward!
Not unobserved, though vainly, to the gods

On silent tablet in their inmost shrines
Suspended she her vows;—for as an oak
On Taurus, or a pine with gummy bark
Torn by a whirlwind from its native rock
Falls headlong down, and with a fearful crash
Spreads ruin far and wide within its track.
So fell the Minotaur by Theseus' hand,
Butting his horns against the empty air.
Then safe and full of honour Theseus came
Back once more to the mouth of that dark den,
Guiding his erring footsteps with a clue
Which Ariadne gave him, lest the maze
Should shut him in for ever in its toils.

Oft, so the tale runs, from the burning depth
Of her sad breast she utter'd piteous plaints,
Oft climb'd the craggy mountain's slippery steep,
To gaze upon the vast expanse of waves.
Or ran among the ripples of the sea
With snowy thighs all bare of covering:
And oft they say that mid her broken sobs
And sighs half choked with tears, she thus
    complain'd:
"Was it for this, false Theseus, thou didst bear
Me from my country and my father's hearth
To leave me thus upon a desert shore?

And dost thou thus, unmindful of thine oath,
With cursèd perjury pollute thy soul?
Could naught to mercy bend thy cruel mind,
Hadst thou no pity left for wretched me?
This, this is not the end thou bad'st me hope,
Nor the fulfilment of the pledge thou gavest;
Thou told'st me then of happy nuptials,
And merry bridal songs and blissful love;
But now thine oaths are sport of all the winds,
Like feathers whirl'd adown the hurricane.
Henceforward let no maid in man believe,
For all his speeches are as false as fair,
And when his end is gain'd, his promises,
Made to deceive, are broken every one.
For though from out the midmost coil of death
By death of mine own kin I rescued thee,
Though rather than forsake thee in thy need
The Minotaur my brother I destroy'd,
Here am I left upon this lonely land
By thee, false man, a prey to beasts and birds;
And when I die upon my whitening bones
No earth shall rest, no hand shall mark the spot,
No human tear bedew my memory!

" What lioness beneath what desert rock
Brought thee into the world, thou ruthless man;

What raging sea from out its foaming waves
Cast thee to shore? what Syrtis gave thee birth,
What ravening Scylla, what Charybdis wild,
Tended thine earliest years,—that thou shouldst give
Such dire reward to her who gave thee life?
If that thou fear'dst our marriage might displease
Thy stern old father the Athenian king,
Yet mightest thou have hid me in some bower
Sacred to thee and me, where day by day
With joyful labour I might toil for thee,
And bring the water for thy weary feet,
Or spread the purple covering on thy couch.—
Yet wherefore to the winds do I complain,
Mad with misfortune? for the winds and seas
Are deaf and cannot understand my moans,—
And he is far away upon the wave,
And help is none upon the lonely strand.
Oh! would that never the Athenian ships
Had cast their anchors on the Gnossian beach;
Would that the treacherous mariner, who brought
The fearful tribute to the savage bull,
To Cretan shore had ne'er his cable bound!
Oh! would that never he whose godlike form
Hid such deceit, had come within our house,
And won my heart, but to destroy me here!"

MAIDENS.

FROM CATULLUS.

AS flower that blooms within some
    guarded grove,—
  Where never ploughshare comes,
    nor cattle graze,—
Foster'd by breeze and shower and sunshine's love,
  Attracts full many a wistful childish gaze,
  But once stem-sever'd loses all its praise,
Nor more to girl or boy seems bright or dear:
  Thus flower-like blooms the maid through kindly
    days,
While chastity enrobes her beauty clear,
But when that flower is lost she claims not one
    poor tear.

THE VISION OF EZEKIEL.

HE Lord's hand was upon me, and He took
Me that hath written all this weary book
Of woes and sorrows;—yea He carried me,
Even as a boat is carried of the sea,
And set me in a valley full of bones:
And round about among the grass and stones,
Leaf-like they lay, like wither'd leaves and dry,—
So dry were they that as the wind pass'd by
Bone upon bone, as boughs of trees on trees,
Rustled, and made a crackling in the breeze,
As dry thorns crackle in the arms of fire,
Harsh to the ear as sound of broken wire
In the mid music stream of Judah's harp:
And through the sky, there roam'd a breath as sharp

As is the breath of him whose prey were these,—
Death, the bleak winter whose embraces freeze
The full warm rush of the blood's stream, and press
The spirit forth of its frail summer dress,
And hurl it into lands of cold and dearth,
Where is no voice of singing nor of mirth,
No sound of tabor, pipe, nor lutestring, more.

Hence, from the land of Babylon He bore
And set me down, and communed with me;
Saying, "O son of man, what dost thou see?"
Then said I, "Bones; and these are very dry."
And the Lord answer'd me, as doth the cry
Of soul that answer unto soul doth give,
" O son of man, and can these slain ones live?"
Then said I, " Lord, there is no man can know,
Save Thou alone." Thereat the blast did blow
Shrill at mine ears, and with it a great cry
Rang thunder-loud around me, " Prophesy,
And say thou thus unto these dead dry bones:
' Though ye be dead, and motionless as stones,
Behold I will lay sinews upon you,
Your flesh shall come again, and the red hue
Of the live blood shall mantle through your frames,
And breath shall come again to you, as flames
Of a dead fire beneath the wind revive,

And soul with breath, and ye shall be alive.'"
And thus I spake, and as I prophesied,
A tremor pass'd through all the valley wide,
A shaking, and the bones together came,
Bone to his bone, and all the bones became
As living men, save that they had no breath—
Pale slumbering men, that doze and dream of death.
Then said he, " Prophesy unto the wind,
And say, ' O wind that breathest o'er mankind,
Through all the skies where the sun journeyeth,
O wind of heaven, hear what thy Maker saith ;
Come from the four far quarters of the earth,
From the dim phantom shores of death and birth,
And breathe upon these slain, that they may live.'"

Then as I spake, as wings of bees that hive
Deep in the forest, fill the leaves with sound
Of fluttering passage, thus upon the ground
The airs of heaven alighted, and the soul
That is as air, roll'd as the tempests roll
Through the dark sky, upon the host of slain,
They breathed and stood upon their feet again,
A living army of exceeding size.
O Lord, how marvellous to our blind eyes
The least of all the wonders of Thine hand,
Yea, deep Thy ways, and hard to understand,

Even from the time Thy word first came to me,
When by the stream of Chebar I did see
Thy glory, and the hand that held the roll,
Which eaten was as honey, and the scroll
Of lamentation, mourning, and long woe:
Even from that time when first Thou bad'st me go,
And speak unto this people in Thy name,
If they perchance would hear me, and proclaim
The heavy punishment of Israel's sin.
Lord, wilt Thou not now turn Thee and begin
In these last days to favour us again,
To work deliverance out of tears and pain,
And bitterness of strange captivity?
Wilt Thou not quicken us once more, and be
As in old time our Father and our King,
And lead us forth like favour'd sheep, and bring
The glory back to sad Jerusalem,
The bud and blossom back to Jesse's stem?
Shall these slain live, and Judah's sceptre fall,
Till Shiloh come, and gather all in all?

THE SCARLET LETTER.

SUGGESTED BY A PICTURE IN THE ROYAL ACADEMY, 1871.

HE prison gates fly open, and I stand
Once more with light and life on either hand,
Once more behold the gladness of the sun,
And know the worst is done that can be done,
The last shame heap'd upon my weary head;
The past a dreary grave that o'er its dead
Shuts like the clang of that vast iron door,
Which closes now behind me, as before
It closed upon the brightness of my life,
And opens but to yield me up to strife
Of mocking tongues, that hate me for my love,
More dearly loved, alas! than heaven above;

The bitter love that was my living death.
Oh God, have mercy, let me but find breath,
Let me but catch one draught of sweet pure air
To still the throb of panting breasts that bear
What never woman bore on earth before:
Oh God, wilt Thou forget to pity more,
Am I cast out for ever from Thy sight,
For that one lingering hour of sweet delight
That were worth heaven to have but once again,
And then descend to depth of endless pain,
And mourn away my spirit through long years
Of deathless grief, and rivers of sad tears:
Where tears shall flow for ever and for ever,
And passion thrill, and love rekindle never?
Oh, love! oh, life! if this my love be sin,
How sweet it is, how sad it is, to win
The last sick joy that waits the swooning soul,
And then be doom'd to torment through the roll
Of never-ending ages of dead space!
Oh God, to whom I may not look for grace
Because my sin is hateful in Thine eye,
Oh! grant me one last boon and let me die;
For better 'twere to fall into Thine hand
Whose mercies are unchanging, than to stand
A scorn and a derision unto men,
And for one sin receive the doom of ten,

In distant looks that coldly turn aside,
And feet that leave my feet a path so wide
I well might be a serpent or a plague.

 How yon ill hag, bow'd down with spleen and age,
Points to the branding letter on my breast,—
My breast, whereon to lie were worth more quest
Than claspings of a thousand meaner arms,—
One wild embrace more worth than all the charms
Of this cold Puritanic human hell,—
One tale of my warm love more sweet to tell
Than records of all fireless frozen days
That these men live with women whose sole praise
Is that they have not loved and sinn'd as I,
Because their hearts are cold like ice; oh! why,
Why should I live an outcast in the sight
Of these that are not bright as I am bright,
Yet flaunt their frigid virtue in my shame,
And laugh with hard thin lips to see my fame
Trod like the very mire under feet?
Shall I be foul to these that are not sweet,
I who am warm and full like ripen'd fruit,
And flush'd with green young life, like some strong shoot
Of clasping foliage of thick tropic vine?
Oh! love, my one sweet love, that still dost shine

My one sole star amid a heaven of gloom,
My one sweet word amid a deadly doom,—
Oh! love, that hast press'd lip to lip with mine
Dost thou not know my lips are strong like wine?
Dost thou not know my arms are fair and full,
And sweet my hair to kiss, and twine, and pull,
Until the bending head droop flower-like down
Upon thy shoulder, mingling white with brown;—
Dost thou not know, my love, how sweet am I?
Oh! better were it both of us should die
Than thou shouldst never feel my soul again
Rush into thine, till pleasure turn'd to pain,
And fluttering sank among the faltering veins,
Till all the heaving spirit's loosen'd chains
Fell from the limbs that quiver'd with delight
Of frame that weaken'd while the soul grew light.
Oh! love whose love lit flame-like at mine eyes,
I know thou wilt not spurn me nor despise,
Because we sinn'd together one sweet sin,
And one poor brittle thread of joy to spin
Gave both our bodies into Satan's hand,
To do his will, and in his temple stand
For ever for one moment of glad sighs,
And full red lips to lips turn'd flower-wise,—
Sad weeping flowers whose fruit should turn t
    pain,

And wheat-like bring forth woe tenfold again,
Wild weary woe, that shall not cease to burn
Here with this letter on my breast, and turn
Love's own abode to deserts parch'd and dry,
Love's summer breeze to breath of wintry sky ;—
Oh! love, I know thou wilt not join to tread
With these upon a bruised and aching head,
Aye well I know thy heart is sore as mine,
And dark thy soul that once did rise and shine
Among the skies, as pure and bright as they
When roselike morning blushes into day.
Oh! love, the pleasure of the deed we wrought
At such dear price was all too dearly bought!
Too dearly say I? Nay; though God and men
Frown on me, I would sin the sin again ;
Aye twenty times, at twenty times the cost,
Nor shed one tear for fame and fortune lost,
Nor heed for aught but that one sweetest thing
That ever wrought twain spirits' ruining.

Away! my thoughts grow wild, my lips blaspheme,
Is all this red disgrace a deadly dream,
A dark unholy vision of the night,
Shall it not fade and dawn to morning bright,
Shall I not wake and find it fled away?
Oh! God, to whom I hardly dare to pray,

Lend me for pity's sake some strength to bear
The brand of this red letter that I wear
Because my feeble soul loved love too well;
Though I should burn in everlasting hell
Let me not shrink and cower before the face
Of these that joy and gloat at my disgrace.
Death! it were better far than such a fate,
Yet for my child would I endure and wait;
Oh! give me strength to look back scorn for scorn,
To live for this the infant I have borne,
That never did one sin in all its days.
Oh! God, whose ways are not as these men's ways
Grant me one grain of mercy for the sake
Of Him that did our earthly nature take,
And knows and feels for our infirmities
Which He hath borne and carried; He who sees
How hard a thing it is for flesh to live
Pure on this vile and spotted earth, and give
No cause of anger to Thy spotless mind:
Who when He dwelt a mortal with mankind
Forgave the many sins of Magdalene.
Oh! God, I ask Thee not to make me clean,
For though repentance could full pardon win
My soul cannot repent of its sweet sin,—
The sweetest sin that e'er was sinn'd, and fain
If it might be would do the same again,

But for my child's sake strengthen me to live,
And spare awhile, if thou canst not forgive.

Pearl, darling Pearl! 'twere worth this load of
    shame
If only once to breathe thy innocent name,
If only once to kiss thee, my sweet child,
And know that though I be a thing defiled
My hands have found, and these my weary knees
Borne thee, the purest pearl of all the seas.

PAST AND PRESENT.

HEN last I trod this ground with thee
The trees were green as now,
The birds were singing merrily
Upon the leafy bough:
The sun was bright, the flowers were gay,
The brook flow'd laughing by,
In the still heaven not a cloud
Obscured the beaming sky.—
And now the place is all unchanged,
It scarcely seems an hour
Since thou and I so joyously
Tripped through the woodland bower.
Oh! we were happy then, and young,
And thou wast, oh! so fair,
But now thou'rt in thy grave, and I
Am left alone with care.
Look down from out the starry heaven,

Look down, blest soul, on me,
And whisper comfort to my soul,
Bereft of love and thee ;
The trees, the birds, the little brook
That ripples to the sea,
Are all the same, but I am changed,
Nor ever more shall be
The thing I was but yesterday,
When thou wast yet with me.

The sea shines bright with spray-dash'd light,
Far out beneath my view,
The trees upon the water's edge
Bend o'er the sheet of blue ;
The waves are murmuring to the shore,
But still my fancy strays
From all the lovely scene around
To those remember'd days,
When hand in hand we wander'd here
Beneath the calm sun's rays.

The grass is green, the sky is blue,
The waves still ripple on,
But all my joy and all my light
Are with thy presence gone.
Oh ! callous sea, how canst thou smile ?

Oh! skies be dim with rain,
For she who fairer was than ye
Is vanish'd, like a strain
Of music, which the longing ear
May never hear again.

LOVE AND WINE.

THE sleepy light of waning night,
　　The pall of winter snows,
The opening rosebud's robe of white,
　　The sparkling wine that flows,
Are fair, but in my lady's hair
　　A richer blossom blows.

Fill up the goblet to the brim,
　　I drink to her and she to me,
And all sad things are far forgotten,
　　And all the ill to be;
Fill high, nor let the Future stain
The Present with one thought of pain.

I love the strong red wine that glows,
　　And laughs, and gleams, and lies,

And like a liquid ruby flows
Among empurpled skies;
But lovelier far to me, the star
Within my lady's eyes.

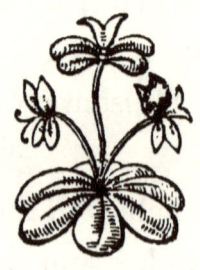

MAUD.

Y little Maud, it's many a day
    Since boy and girl together
We play'd at love, and loved in play,
    Two birds of callow feather.

But I'm no chicken now, alas!
    For Time will stay for no man,
And years have changed the sprightly lass
    Into a charming woman.

Now if we meet and find some day,
    All childish love departed,
Why let us set to work and play,
    And go our ways whole hearted.

But if we take to love again
    Don't let us take to playing,
Play's out of place in harvest time
    Though very well in Maying.

WANDERING FIRES.

VER the lonely moorland wastes
    When the sinking twilight dies,
  The Will-o'-the-wisp with flickering flame,
Glimmers, and flits, and flies.

Calm on the waves of the midnight sea
    The shimmering moonbeams play,
Glittering over the watery waste,
    Over the whitening spray:

Quivering, glancing, gliding along,
    They share in the ceaseless motion
Of the clouds that reflect their endless change
    On the ever changing ocean.

And so with the fires of Life's young morn;
  They sparkle, and gleam, and die,
Changing as change the shadow scenes
  In the vault of the summer sky.

The hopes that we cherish'd long ago,
  Where are they now! oh! where?
Vanish'd more quickly than drops of dew
  Into the morning air.

The transient gleams of loves and dreams
  Unstable as wandering fires
Pass by, and our youthful passions die,
  Burnt up by their own desires,
On splendid perfumed funeral piles
  On regal and odorous pyres.—
And we gather the ashes, and close the urn,
When the spectral flames have ceased to burn.

And our life is a fire that blazes awhile,
  Then sinks and is gulf'd in the gloom
That broods before Death's murky door,
  Hiding the shapes in the Future's womb;
Like the Will-o'-the-wisp while ye may then play,
  For the end of your play is the tomb.

THE OWL.

Set to Music by W. Harrison, Esq.

ROAM by night in the pale moonlight,
    Merry and fearless and free,
When the stars above are shining bright,
    Ho! that's the time for me.

'Tis then I flit through the dark pine grove,
    Through the dark pine grove I fly,
In the day I rest, but at night I rove,
    And hoot with joyful cry.

Full merry's my song as I glide along,
    In the night alone I see,
I hate the day with its noisy throng,
    But night's the time for me!

THE BAT.

MEN may prate of the brightness of day,
    And the joy of the sunbeams' play,
    Of love, and of light, and of morn,
    But the hours from twilight to dawn
To the grey bat are gladder than these,
And ivy and sombre yew trees,
Gayer than fountain and lawn.
Ho! merry's the night and the gloaming grim,
When the bat flies forth as the day grows dim.

    Over the world as it sleeps,
    Swift through the mist as it creeps
    Ghostily up from the breast
    Of the churchyard, where still and at rest
    Lieth the dead in his shroud,
    Flieth the bat like a cloud.
    Men deem him lonely and sad,

Think ye his heart is not glad?
Ho! 'tis a right merry jest.
For gay is the night and the gloaming grim,
When the bat flies forth as the day grows dim.

Then hurrah! for the bat and his life,
And hurrah! for his spectral wife,
Who sits in her murky bower,
In the heart of the old church-tower;
And hurrah! for their weird wild play,
Mirth ends not with ending of day,
For night is as joyous as morn,
And twilight as gladsome as dawn.
Then ho! waken up, and away,
For merry's the night and the gloaming grim,
When the bat flies forth as the day grows dim.

A VALENTINE.

SWEET Jessie, St. Valentine's day
Is come now, and what shall I say,
As I take up my long unused pen,
To write and to rhyme once again;
Shall I tell you your eyes are as bright
As the flash of some strange meteor's light—
As the mist that awakens to dew
In the cup of a violet blue,
Shall this be my message to you?

Shall I tell you your bosom is white
As the snow 'neath the Polar star's light
When the Arctic night blushes to dawn;
That your breath is as odour of roses
Ere the bud into blossom uncloses,
As twilight recedes into morn.

A VALENTINE.

Shall I tell you your lips are as sweet
As honey by bees at the feet
Of Mount Hybla, close gather'd and stored,
In the time when Olympus was still
The abode of the gods, and each hill
Had its nymph, and each river its lord?

Shall I liken your voice to low chords
Of music, your glances to swords,
With the fire of Anacreon of old,
Whose lyre but of love sang and told?
Nay, the hand of such harpers is cold—
There is none now can sing as he sung;
And the lays of Catullus are flung
Aside as too warm and too bold.

And as others around me, not I,
In verses will pule, rave, and lie,
Then what shall I say to my love
Shall be pure as the heaven above,
And sweet as the breath of the South,
Or the kiss of her own rosy mouth,
Do I know?—Can I tell?—No, not I.

If aught can be sweeter than love,
I still have that sweetness to prove;

A VALENTINE.

Though my song and my verse may be weak
There are feelings the lips cannot speak,
So sweet, I can offer but Love;
He comes from the regions above,
He is white as a pale lily's bloom
That hangs o'er a young maiden's tomb.
Then take him and wear him, my sweet,
While youth lasts, for full fleet are his feet;
He is here for a moment, then gone—
And swift is the rush of his wing
As the birth and the death of the spring,
And the songs of the seasons that sing
   As the years journey on.

SONG. IN THE FOREST.

N the deepest, shadiest forest,
   Where the grasses greenest be,
   Where the summer breezes softest
   Murmur from the distant sea;
Where in low monotony,
Wandering stream and bird
Sing the whole midsummer day,
Fairy voice is heard,
Fairy fancies while away
Weary toiler into play.

Where the bluest harebells drooping,
Hide among long fronds of fern
Lover-like above them stooping,
Where the noon sun cannot burn,

SONG. IN THE FOREST.

From the thirsty noonday turn,
On the mossy carpet lie,
See the light peep through the boughs,
Peep from crystal dome of sky
Where is naught to rouse;
Naught to tell of noise and riot,
Nothing but supremest quiet.

Where the darkest ivy twines
Round and round the stateliest stems.
Where the glossy holly shines,
Where the violet's gems
Starlike peer through heaven of green,
There are fairest phantoms seen,
Phantom voices whisper verse,
Heart becomes as universe;
In deep woods, if anywhere,
Aching brows forget their care.

Where the timorous ring-dove calling
Softest woos his willing mate,
Eloquence of Silence falling
Spirit soothes, world-desolate.
One companion, only one,
Her thou lovest, take with thee,

SONG. IN THE FOREST.

Where the tiniest squirrels run,
Freest roams the bee;
In the forest's boundless leisure
There is Love a double pleasure.

Hast thou none to love and cherish?
Take thy thoughts alone with thee.
Finest feelings often perish
Lacking perfect harmony:
Trouble not the woodland sea
With the idle words of men,
There alone tranquillity,
Undisturb'd repose should be,—
Gaze, depart, come back again.

SONG. LOST LOVE.

DREARILY, drearily, moans the wind
    Through the boughs of the old elm
        tree,
    Drearily, drearily, sweeps the storm
O'er the face of the swelling sea;
But still more drearily cometh the thought
    Of the Future unto me.

Sadly, oh! sadly sigh the birds
    In the branches thin and bare,
While ever and aye the ceaseless snow
    Falls through the freezing air;
But sadder and colder is the load
    This weary heart must bear.

Quickly, oh! quickly fade the flowers,
    When summer's reign is o'er,

SONG. LOST LOVE.

Leafless and bare are the once gay bowers,
    Which late such verdure bore;
Yet the flowers shall return with the April showers,
    But Hope to me no more.

Mournfully sighs the desolate breeze,
    Under the window pane,
Sadly it rustles among the trees,
    In the midst of the snow and rain:
Yet Spring will soon come to the wakening earth,
    But Love to me never again.

LIFE.

E live and we love in a dream here on
   earth,
   And we know not what is to come;
   Our moments fly fast to the days
      that are past,
Like a bird to its leaf-bower'd home.

We scheme and we purpose our doings to-day,
   But all is chang'd on the morrow,
Hope's moon may shine bright through the starry
      night,
   The morn may bring nothing but sorrow.

Our life is the bloom on a butterfly's wing,
   The haze on a mist of the morn,
The voice of the newly awakened Spring,
   The joy of the early dawn ;—

All passes away, like the beams that play
    On the waves of some glittering stream ;
What seemeth so fair and lovely to-day
    Will soon be the joy of a dream.

Oh! Love thou art fleeting, oh! Life thou art sad.
    Oh! Years ye are buried in gloom;
Oh! would that the music of life's young morn
    Might awake from its early tomb.

Vain longing! what is to be shall, and thou art
    The thing that thou shalt be and must,
And the yearnings that once fill'd thine innermost heart,
    Are crumbled away into dust.

And that heart which once thrill'd to the voiceless flame
    Of Poesy now is still :
The emotions that were are now naught but a name,
    And nothing their place may fill.

Oh! world, there are many that think thee real,
    I surely thine emptiness know ;

LIFE.

Fade, fade into air, thou fleeting strain,
   And dissolve in the winds that blow;
Let thy dying notes wail o'er the days that are dead,
   In a melody soft and low.

SINGING.

HE song I sung in bygone days
    I sing again to-day,
But from the idle notes and words
    My thoughts are far away.

Methinks I live in perish'd times
    And sing that song again;
And bending o'er me see a face,
    Which now to see were pain.

And hear a voice in tones as sweet
    As music breathing low;
And speech from lips which press'd to mine
    Once set my heart aglow.

Methinks I see her lovely face
    Change with the music's change,
As every note within her heart
    Stirr'd feelings new and strange.

Methinks I feel the nameless thrill
    That whisper'd then to me,
" She knoweth that thou lovest her,
    And she too loveth thee."

Ah! fool, she is another's bride,
    Another clasps her hand,
Another standeth by her side,
    Where thou wast wont to stand.

The vision fades, and now my eyes
    With tears begin to fill,
I turn me to the notes again,
    But memory haunts me still.

I sing; the notes come clear and full,
    And answer each endeavour,
But there's a something in the strain
    Has gone from me for ever.

TO ONE DEPARTED.

THOU wast a soul within my soul,
   An isle in life's rough sea,
A sweet draught in the gilded bowl
   Of being pure and free;
A refuge from the tempest's roll,
   Oh! love, my love, to me!

Now weary days and weary years
   Must be my lot for ever,
Each morn be wet with fruitless tears,
   And life from Hope dissever;
For what hath been shall now be seen
   By me, ah! never, never!

The grass is green upon thy grave
   Beside the mountain stream;

A gem in every tiny wave
    Glows in the mid-day gleam,
And o'er thy head the branches wave
    Like phantoms in a dream.

My darling I am all alone,
    No more, no more, no more
Shall float thy tresses zephyr-blown
    Along the windy shore!
No more thy voice bid soul rejoice
    Wounded and weak and sore!

Ah! never, never more, thou art
    On a throne in the heaven on high,
Yet still thine image in my heart
    As in a lake doth lie,—
As in the air soft waves of prayer
    In music burst and die.

Yet still when through the darkening sky
    The pale moon upward gleams,
And at early morn, when dawn is nigh,
    I see thee in my dreams;
And on thy face with a deathless grace
    The light of glory beams.

LOVE'S COMPARISONS.

WHAT is like thee? oh! say what is
    like thee;
  Is it the cloudy rainbow's pearliest
    hue?
Is it the purple haze of dying sunlight?
  Is it the noonday heaven's spotless blue?

Is it the rill that murmurs through the forest,
  Bubbling and sparkling on its mossy bed?
Is it a flower that with the dawn of daylight
  Towards the sky uplifts its odorous head?

Is it the inspiration of a poet,
  Pouring his accents in a crystal strain?
Is it the rosy blushing red of autumn?
  Is it the gentle spring-time's earliest rain?

Is it a nightingale at even singing,
　　Loud, clear, and shrill?
Is it the vesper bell's melodious ringing,
　　Breaking in silver waves behind the hill?
Is it the requiem of one departed,
　　Solemn and still?

Is it the love that words can never utter
　　Of all that's beautiful and good and true?
Is it the lustre of a priceless jewel?
　　Is it a valley lily wet with dew?

Tell me, oh! tell me, for alone thou knowest
　　What is like thee:
Eyes dazzled by the lustre of thy beauty
　　Nothing else can see;
So unless thou tell me,
　　I must silent be.

TO ——. WITH A CAMELLIA.

DEAR girl, accept this flower from me,
    'Tis fair, but not so fair as thou,
For every time thy face I see
    New beauties crown thee queen, as now.

The flower is fair, but not like thee,
    By morning it will fade away,
While all the many charms we see
    In thee grow lovelier day by day.

Its gaudy leaves are scentless all,
    But thou art sweet as is the rose,
Other delights the sense may pall,
    Thy sweetness ever sweeter grows.

TO ———. WITH A CAMELLIA.

'Tis winter-time, and in our clime
   Of frosts and snows few flowers will bloom,
Until once more the glad spring-time
   Scatters old Winter's cold and gloom:

But thou art blooming all the year,
   For ever young, and fair, and bright,
Oh! would that I could plant thee here,
   To grow for ever in my sight.

SONNET. TO THE SISTER NIGHTINGALES.

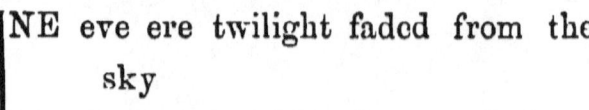NE eve ere twilight faded from the sky
A wanderer stray'd adown a darkening grove,
And heard a nightingale that sang, like Love,
Deep in the heart of man, and then flew by.
And as he walk'd and thought, his mind grew sad,
That he should never hear her music more
Knock softly, sweetly, at his spirit's door,
In melancholy that to him was glad.
   Methinks I have more cause to mourn than he,
More cause for heavy heart and thoughts of sorrow,
For fairer nightingales will fly to-morrow,
And songless leave the empty grove to me.—
Farewell! sweet sisters; though we meet no more,
Bright stars within my midnight will ye be.

CLARA.

THERE is no help for him whose hope
    is dead,
As mine lies dead that died for love
    of you ;
By him alike the false thing and the true,
Beauty or fame, are little coveted ;
There are no pillows for the weary head
That hath forgot the fashion of desire,
And no more feels the flame of longing fire
The soul whose essence is shed out, like dew
That vanishes beneath the noon-sun's rays,
And knows not of the day if it be bright,
And knows not night, nor visions of the night,
Nor work, nor leisure, labour-time, nor play,
But as my soul, that perish'd in thy light,
Flies high in air, and weeps itself away.

THE GARDEN OF LOVE.

AST season when this day came round
   A gay and gaudy garden grew
   Where now dead leaves of hopes
      bestrew
The sad uncultivated ground.

The old hopes budded, bloom'd and died,
   A barren crop that left no seed;
   No dream that shaped itself in deed,
No longing that was satisfied.

He that sows nothing shall reap wind,
   He that sows hope shall reap despair,
   For seldom is the fruit as fair
As is the vision of the mind.

My seeds of hope were dried and dead,
   My young plants wither'd in the sun,
   And now the reaping time is done,
And not a grain is harvested.

THE GARDEN OF LOVE.

I planted all the plot with love,
   But not one seed has taken root;
   On sapless stem and leafless shoot
The mocking sunshine smiles above.

Few things there be that end aright
   Upon this sterile, crooked earth,
   Few seeds that flourish and give birth
From fading flower to fruit as bright.

This year shall pass as others pass'd,
   ·But on its seedless soil, I fear,
   Shall naught be cast save some stray tear,
Till tears shall cease to fall at last.

LITTLE FLO COLBURN.

LITTLE Flo Colburn, tiny Flo,
Where have you gone, dear? why did you go?
You've taken my heart, and I can't tell when
Or how I shall get it back again.

A month ago I came to the sea,
As fancy free as the seabirds be,
That wildly sweep o'er the fetterless foam
Of the whitening waves of their world-wide home.

But Love takes tribute of all, and we
In vain from his subtle thraldom flee,
He is swift and cruel and keen as fate,
Though he seem to pause and falter and wait.

And long though the pitcher go to the well,
One day there's a different tale to tell;
And to Love men's hearts are but vessels of clay,
In the heedless grasp of a child at play.

One gets crack'd in a minute, and one
Lasts till the half of the game is done,
But hard indeed must the fabric be,
That passes the hands of the imp scot free.

He left my heart alone for a while,
Then turn'd at last with a mischievous smile,
Chipp'd it a little against a stone,
Pass'd to another, and left it alone;

And I flatter'd myself it would find its way
Not much the worse through the rough horse-play;
But now, alas! he has taken the crock,
And dash'd it full at a granite rock.

Little Flo Colburn, you were the rock,
My frail heart shiver'd to shreds at the shock,
You glanced where the glittering fragments lay,
Gather'd the pieces, and took them away.

I met you,—yes, I remember it well,
In the large saloon of the new hotel ;—
The dearest, funniest, tiniest thing
That ever was born without butterfly wing.

You look'd half lost in the great strange place,—
A fairy creature of silk and lace,
With the clearest, roundest, blue-black eyes,
Deep as the calm of the Northern skies.

We soon got acquainted, and day after day
Walk'd and rode and sail'd on the bay,
Scrambled over the cliffs for flowers,
Lent new wings to the flying hours.

Ah! Time flies fast when men wish him to stay,
Snail-like crawls when they wish him away,
And Time flew fast with you and with me,
Little Flo Colburn, there by the sea.

You sang like an angel, fairy Flo,
Strange old melodies rich and low,
And I sat listening deep in a dream,
Fitting a verse to the music's stream.

Do you ever think of the rhymes I made,
As I remember each note you play'd?
Do you ever waste as the moments flee,
One small thought on my songs and me?

I wonder whether you liked me, Flo?—
Queer fish we poets are, you know,
Our heads are full of the strangest things,
Honey and love, and stings and wings;

Thoughts of pleasure, and thoughts of pain,
Elfin lands, and castles in Spain,
Gloom and sunshine, winds and snows,
And dreams too wild for sensible prose.

I tried to show you the things that lie
Far out of sight of the careless eye,
The swell and the fall of the mighty verse
That wells from the soul of the Universe;—

From every flower and bird and tree,
From the sealike clouds, and the cloudy sea,
The " sermons in stones " that the poet hears,
The thoughts that lurk, " too deep for tears."

Did you think me an aimless dreamer, Flo,
A feather that every wind might blow
This way and that? yet I sometimes thought
You saw the meaning my poor words taught.

It may be you did, or did not; but now
Little it matters anyhow;
Little indeed,—we have said Goodbye
For ever, I fancy, you and I.

Before you went I liked you only,
But somehow the place look'd dull and lonely,
Sad as a corpse when the spirit has flown,
Flo, little Flo, when you were gone.

I roam'd about in a listless mood,
Down to the sea, and up to the wood,
Into the town, and back again,
Till the sense of emptiness verged on pain.

I tried not to think of you, Flo, but in vain,
Your image was stamp'd as with fire on my brain,
I knew that I loved you now you were gone,
And I love you more as the days pass on.

It's a whole week now since you went, and I stand
Where we often stood, on the belt of sand
Under the cliffs, and the water's sigh
Sounds like the voice of the days gone by.

Little Flo Colburn, here by the sea,
The sea breeze whispers a thing to me,
I shall see you while tides shall flow to the shore,
Little Flo Colburn, never more.

While waves shall ebb from the strand to the main,
Little Flo Colburn, never again
Shall I see the blue of the waves and skies,
Shine back in the blue of your deep dark eyes.

And now in the lull of the noonday air
The breeze that ruffled your violet hair
But a week ago, blows over to me,
Though the hours that were no more shall be;—

The breeze is the same, and the sun, and the sky,
For Nature is changeless and passeth not by,
Oh! for the vanish'd light and grace
Of little Flo Colburn's fairy face.

Darling, while you were here and near,
I never guess'd you were half so dear,
And now I shall see you, come joy, come pain,
Little Flo Colburn, never again.

"Never again!" the murmurous sea
Moaneth in syllables sad to me;
"Never more, oh! never more,"
Sighs the wind through the trees on the shore.

Little Flo Colburn, why did you go?
Did you never guess, did you never know
The love that my own heart scarcely knew,
Sea-deep hidden, yet tender and true?

Little Flo Colburn, many a day
I shall see your face in the glass of the bay,
I shall hear your voice when the sea winds blow,
Little Flo Colburn, faint and low.

I shall see your form in a noonday dream,
And hear your song in the song of the stream,
And fancy I hear as I would full fain
Little Flo Colburn singing again.

Your songs will fall upon other ears,
Your heart for another know pleasures and fears ;
I never told you I loved you at all,
And the days that are gone are beyond recall.

The Past is gone to the dead Past's grave,
From the wreck of a life there's little to save,
I have let you go,—no more can be said
Of the greatest blunder I ever made.

Little Flo Colburn, Time and Fate
Wail together " Too late ! Too late !"
The dirge of Hope, and the funeral knell
Of the "Might have been," that we love so well.

Little Flo Colburn, you and I,
While days on days fast come, fast fly,
Shall stand as we stood on the blue bay's shore,
Where the yellow gorse flowers bloom, no more.

We shall walk no more as we walk'd before
On the terraced cliffs above the shore,
Watching the glittering mirror below,—
Little Flo Colburn, why did you go ?

I wonder what you are doing now,
What you are thinking or speaking of,—how
The hair falls over your neck, like night
On a world of snowfields wild and white.

Little Flo Colburn, night and day
Wearily drag now you are away,
For this is the worst of all sorrowful things,
That Time grief-laden forgetteth his wings.

And at dawn I remember the light of your eyes,
And the sun of your smile with the midday skies,
And twilight tells of your wandering hair,
Heavy with perfume strange and rare.

Well, all flirtations must come to an end,
And life and the years we squander or spend,
For love sinks back like the ebbing wave,
And life like a shallop sails to the grave;
But the ebb of the tide of my life will be low
When you are forgotten, my fairy Flo.

MY LOVES.

WHEN I was but a boy, love,
    A love before me stood,
  Wreathed round with tears and joy, love,
    And lilies for a hood;
When I was but a boy, love,
    This love before me stood.

When I grew up a man, love,
    My love was like the rose,
That kissing breezes fan, love,
    Till every leaf unclose;
When I grew up a man, love,
    Nor dreamt of age's snows.

A love of later life, love,
    Bent over me and sigh'd,

Of passion and of strife, love,
    Sigh'd, flicker'd, flamed and died;
This love of later life, love,
    That might not long abide.

And now there's little left, love,
    Of passion's golden thread,
To weave withal a weft, love,
    For youthful loves are fled:
Then who has done this theft, love,
    And who has stol'n the thread?

Who, who? Why you're the thief, love,
    That steals my love away,
Then take, but bring not grief, love,
    Nor pain instead of play,
For then were no relief, love,
    No dawn of brighter day:

No downy couch of snows, love,
    Where coming age might sleep,
And swoon in long repose, love,
    Nor wake to laugh or weep,
No arms where love might doze, love,
    And dream away his sleep:

MY LOVES.

No poppy love of rest, love,
    That neither fires nor chills,
No end of weary quest, love,
    Among life's vales and hills,
Of flying, dying rest, love,
    That neither feeds nor fills.

I lie within your arms, love,
    And dream and doze awhile,
I feed on all your charms, love,
    And sport upon your smile,
Nor heed for past alarms, love,
    But bask within your smile.

I know not what shall come, love,
    It may be mirth or pain,
But thou'rt my summer home, love,
    And thou my autumn rain;
Then no more will I roam, love,
    While love shall wax and wane.

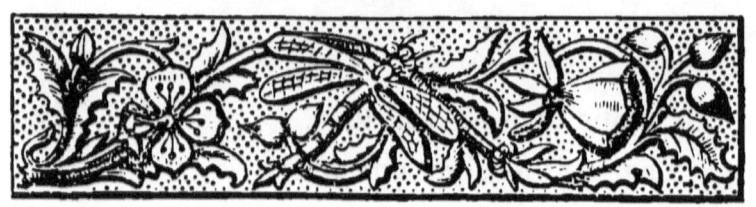

LADY MAY.

MY Lady May, my darling,
    My thoughts wing back to you,
As with the spring the starling
    That heralds skies of blue:
Yet streams and skies and sunbeams,
    On banks of green astray,
Are not so fair as your bright hair,
    My lovely Lady May.

All sweetest songs and voices
    That earth gives back to heaven,
When bird and bee rejoices,
    And one day lives like seven,
Lives, laughs, and smiles, and closes,
    Waves hands as fain to stay,
And lie like loves on roses,
    Or through sweet gardens stray,

Have not one wile of your least smile,
　　My darling Lady May.

The long blue glass of ocean
　　That lies asleep in dreams
Of low and lazy motion,
　　And murmur of hush'd streams,
That woo the soul to slumber
　　Adown the dozing day,
When visions know no number,
　　And pains release their prey,
For all its light is not so bright
　　As you, my Lady May.

The wisdom of the silence
　　That flows through heaven's wide way,
When stars shine out like islands
　　In worlds and wastes of grey;
When spirit speaks to spirit,
　　And thoughts like moonbeams stray
And gaze on eyes of mildest skies
　　That smile their souls away,
Is lowlier heard than your least word,
　　My darling Lady May.

M

THE DAYS OF THE YEARS OF OUR PILGRIMAGE.

H! days of light, oh! days of dancing
    hours,
  Oh! days when no wind blows nor
    storm cloud lowers,
How bright your hours, how bright, oh! days, and
  fleet,
Oh! days of light, oh! days too short, too sweet.

Oh! days of gloom, oh! days of clouded skies,
Oh! days of heavens that weep like heavy eyes,
How long your wingless hours, how cold, how
  sad,
Oh! days of gloom when not a thought was
  glad.

Oh! mingled days, oh! days of shine and shower,
Oh! days when storm and sun alike have power,
Too few, alas! too few your hours of light,
Too long your leaden weighted hours of night!

Oh! days of youth, oh! long-remember'd days,
Oh! days of careless hours and flowery ways,
How soon is all your sunny pastime fled,
Fled, to return no more till time be dead!

Oh! days of love, oh! days of mirth and pain,
Oh! days of fruitful life and love life's bane,
How soon is all your dream-play past away,
As dreams at dawn that vanish into day!

Oh! days of age, oh! looming days of sorrow,
That ever nearer come with each to-morrow,
Have ye no pity for the whitening head
Whose crown of thorns ye twine with loved things
    fled?

Oh! days when life shall be an ended tale,
Oh! days of death and death's wild shadowy vale.
Shall rest or toil be burden of your song,
Waste work that wakes, or slumber deep and long?

MORNING, NOON, AND NIGHT.

HERE was a morning when my heart was light
With youthful presage of untried delight,
There was an hour when fields and flowers were fair
To careless mind that never dreamt of care:
But now, alas! those times have pass'd away,
    This many a day.

There was a noon when Love drew nigh to me,
And his soft voice was as a melody
That ebbs and swells, and haunts the ear in dreams
Of rippling music, and cool rippling streams;
But now, alas! the echo of his lay
    Has pass'd away.

There was an evening when the ghost of Fame
Sprung from the ashes of a quenchless flame
That through the day had seared my heart to stone:
Then said I, " Life is sweet for Fame alone ;"
Alas! the wraith was but wild shadow-play
  Of darkening day.

There is a night shall come, we know not when,
To every soul that wakes and weeps with men,
But shall there any beam break through the night,
From eyes of her that was my spirit's light,
My guardian star, whose dim and distant ray
  Has waned away?

DESOLATION.

FAR, far away the sun below the west
    Sets into night:
Far, far away the voice of days for-
    gotten
Like snow falls light ;—
Like winds on desert waves,
Or thoughts but half begotten,
    Or wandering dream-births, drest
In hues of Fancy's painting,
That faint with daylight fainting,
    And sunlike sink to rest.

Oh! day, and wilt thou fly,
Oh! voices, will ye die,
Oh! hours, that haste to waste away
Why flee so fast, oh! why?
For in the rhyme of being

DESOLATION.

All lovely chords fast fleeing
Depart, all sights worth seeing
   Grow pale with passing day.

As dim death life surprises,
   So on the flickering ray
Of day the nightstar rises,
   In ghostly garments grey
Of clouds, that float and wander
Below the moon, beyond her,
To western seas where yonder,
   Wild twilight shadows stray.

And here where sands are glowing
   In wan and waning light,
Where dark waves ebbing, flowing,
Sway with the breezes' blowing,
Long sounds of oxen lowing,
   Float seawards with the night;

And here where seas are sighing,
   In sleepy fitful tone,
Weak wandering voices crying
Die with dim daylight dying,
And mourn with sunlight flying,
   And with waste waters moan;

DESOLATION.

And here where waves are foaming,
   'Neath gusts that rave and rouse
Dull spectral cloud-sprites roaming
Adown the grim grey gloaming,
As if dark Night were combing
   Dark hair across wan brows;

I stand with wet eyes weeping,
   And breast that beats in pain,
And watch the twilight creeping
Among the heavens, and sleeping
Above black waves, that leaping
   Wax white on watery plain.

And while like wild swan's singing
   My soul is lost in air,
Sad restless thoughts flit winging,—
While latest light is flinging
Weird crimson tints, and bringing
   Lost dreams of days more fair—

Like rays from red sun darted,
   To singing hours now dumb:
Ere love from life was parted,
Ere soul sobb'd, broken-hearted,
" Alas! the day departed,
   " Alas! the night to come."

A FAREWELL.

FAREWELL to the sorrow and sadness,
   The joy and the tremulous pain,
   Farewell to the grief and the gladness
   Of love that shall live not again;
Farewell to the rhyme and the measure,
   The notes of the music of youth,
Farewell to the tears and the treasure
   Of harvested truth.

Farewell to the face that was dearest
   To me of all faces that smile,
Farewell to the heart that beat nearest
   The heart of my heart for a while;
Farewell to the moon of my darkness,
   The lamp and the light of my soul,
Which now through years trackless and sparkless
   Must grope to its goal.

Turn hither one moment ere flying
  My soul shall collapse into night;
Let me catch thy last ray ere its dying
  Rob living of life and of light:
From the wealth of thy days grant one hour
  To one that will weep at its close,
While the sun in the summer hath power,
  In winter the snows.

Thou art blest with an infinite blessing,
  The warmth and the worship of love,
Oh! bloom of the sunwind's caressing,
  Bend hither thy head from above:
Bend hither and smile as in pity
  On the dull rugged cypress that sighs
To the sound of the mournful wind's ditty,
  That stirs it, and flies.

Thou spreadest thy leaves in the daytime
  Of love, and affection, and life;
Through his boughs the wild storm hath its play-
      time,
  The snows sing their music of strife:
The rains rush in ruinous laughter
  From the twigs to the blast-bitten stem,
The waste grass at his dead roots hereafter
  Shall no dew begem.

A FAREWELL.

Bend hither one moment, then flourish
    For others, and shine from afar,
Thy scent sweet remembrance shall nourish
    Thou flower, thy radiance, oh, star!
Shall burst through the midnight of being,
    Through the gloom give one glimmer of light,
Grow strong while faint eyes swim in seeing,
    Oh! moon of my night.

NEW YEAR'S SONG.

THE old year dies, the new year breathes
   Glad perfume as of bursting leaves,
    Clear streams, and songs of many
      birds,
And voices of awakening hours
Of spring, and feathery falling showers,
   And eloquence of speechless words.

O Man, the old year droops and dies,
The new year brings new sweets,—Arise
   New-born, and leave the past behind;
Leave superstition, hate, and fears,
And weak regrets, and weaker tears,
   Dull ignorance, and folly blind.

NEW YEAR'S SONG.

Awake to new and loftier life,
Press onward in a nobler strife,
   Reach forward to a greater prize,
Set God alone before thine eyes;
Not man, nor aught of man's device
   That leads and lures, not satisfies.

Break down the proud priest's impious throne,
Revere not man but God alone;
   Go not with those that rave and cry,
" Lo here, lo there, is right or wrong;"
Pause not to hear their Syren song
   That prates of life,—for these shall die.

Lift up thine eyes to that blue sky
That shines above thee lovingly,
   Look once around, then dare to say,
Yea, if thou canst, " Lo these are vile;"
Bask in thy fellow creature's smile,
   Then say, " All these have gone astray."

Leave narrow views to feed the past,
Leave bigotry to breathe its last,
   Leave foolish creeds to wax and wane;
With the old year let all darkness die,
With the new year let the sun rise high,
   Learn not and labour not in vain.

Go on, O Man! from strength to strength
With each new season, till at length
  Thou shalt stand under the free sky,
And see all clouds and fears decay,
All old world follies pass away,
  Truth reign alone, and error fly.

SONG.

H! land of life, wherein this soul of ours,
   Like living air among thy many trees
After sweet rain, from leaves of greenest bowers
Shakes down sad drops of sorrow-laden showers,
   That weep along the winds of sullen seas:

Oh! land of flowers, oh! gauzy land of ours,
   Oh! bubble that like mirrors of the moon
Dost glass far cloudy forms of cloudy towers,
Oh! butterfly of short and sunny hours,
   Oh! morning mist that meltest with the noon:

Oh! land of life, my lady is as thou,
   And as thy wind the whisper of her breath,

And as thy trees the tresses of her brow,
And as thy sun that sinks in twilight now
   Her smile, and as thy voice the words she saith.

Ah! sweet as showers of spring are her sweet tears,
   When Love that hovers round the labouring
      breast
As compass needle round the dial veers,
Points now to South of sighs,—to North of fears,
   Till Hope the magnet draw it into rest.

Sing, all ye flowers, in scented harmony,
   Oh, sunlight! wander through her window-pane,
And love-soft let your silent message be,
Bid her sleep light, and sleeping dream of me,
   Then with the morning wake for me again.

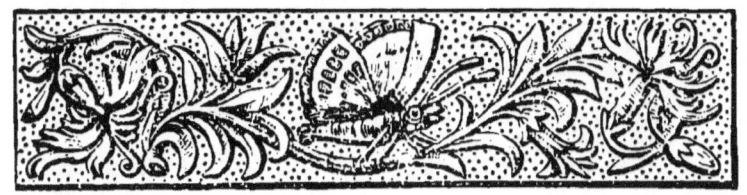

A FLOWER PHANTASY.

THERE is a garden in a sunny vale,
Deep in the silence of the dreamy hills
That girdle round an isle of Fairy
 land;
Through which one day I wander'd listlessly
O'er flowery slopes by side of whispering stream,
Where blooms the rose, that like an amorous soul
Opens its leaves to catch the wind's embrace,
And breeds there from red heavy perfumed airs,
That plume their drowsy wings, and brood, and lie
Full in the swooning sunlight, or moist breath
Of evening, when the subtle scent pervades
The solemn aisles of dim mysterious trees,
Where shady phantasies of twilight dwell,
Foreshadowings and forebodings of the land
Whose name is Twilight, and whose noon is
 night;—
Lilies that droop in cold virginity,

And muse of drifts of snows, and drifting foam,
That like the light ghost of the thundering floods
Floats uppermost, and reaches out to heaven,
And goes men know not whither:—tulips gay
As is the broad mirth of an August day,
The worldlings of the wilderness of flowers,
That live and reck not of hereafter storms:—
Violets, that like a young bride hang their heads,
That grows more lovely out of very shame
At her own sweet delight, and wondrous store
Of hoarded pleasure met in secret ways
With the night's dew and silent stars alone,
And one sole heart for witness:—hyacinths,
That from the sky have stolen, Prometheus-like,
The blue of all their buds, that through the leaves
Heap blue on green, as in September days
The cloud-god hangs his fleeces in the sky,
And dyes them with the colours of the bow:
Pale stephanotis with its creamy bloom,
Aud scent that is as savour of sweet song,
And gratitude begotten of good deeds
That ever bring back interest:—clematis,
That clasps and clothes and hides like charity,
And ivy leaves that shine in Slumber's hair,
Dreaming of night in daytime:—orange bloom,
Rich with blithe memories of wedding bells,

And tender garner'd joys, and tenderer pain :—
Geraniums that wither in their morn,
As man, and as the passion of his breast;
White, as the loves of early youth, and red
With fears, and shame, and sin, and tears of blood,
As are the wandering loves of later years,
When the ideal lies all crush'd and torn,
Besmirch'd with mud, and soil'd with miry clay
Of many a fleshly quagmire; dull sad pink
As are the lukewarm loves of childish age,
And mottled, as the spirit that is led,
Now here, now there, now spreading wings to soar,
Now wallowing contented on the ground :—
Snowdrops that are as hope amid despair,
And crocuses as fragile as man's will,
That every gust of chance may break and mar ;—
Sharp cherry scent, and smells of heather bloom,
That like good counsel cheer the fainting soul,
And vines that like an angel woman's love
Cling still through storm and rain, nor loose their
    hold
Till Death's sharp sickle shear the stems in
    twain :—
Fierce peonies whose days are brief and full,
Whose crimson petals glow with sensuous gleam,
Even as the breast that heaves, and feeds on love,

And flame-lit eyes, and Joy that laughs and flies,
And leaves the heart to pine for what is gone
With the gone years, and may not turn again,
Though flesh and spirit crumble into dust,
As doth the Sodom apple in the grasp
Of hungry traveller, that fain would taste
What seems so warmly vein'd with luscious juice,
Yet turns to shreds and ashes at his lips:—
Long tendrils of the trailing honeysuckle,
That like Remembrance springs from hidden roots,
So tangled that we scarce can follow them
To their first source:—soft peaches and sleek
    plums,
And waxwork of the deep pomegranate flower.

Then came there one that was as my first love,
And led my steps among the many paths,
Until we came to where a little plot
Was strangely set with ill-assorted flowers ;
And then she turn'd her eyes upon mine eyes
And said, " Behold the garden of men's days,
And in this plot the fashion of thy life."

Then as I look'd the flowers were dark and light,
And all the ground was matted thick with weeds,
And round red rose stems ragged bindweed twined,

And there was stephanotis set for song,
And leaves of wither'd snowdrops waste and dead,
And sprigs of box, and stunted cypress shrubs,
'Mong which long threads of prickly brier
 crawl'd,
And through the wild, as through the misty sky,
A wealth of choked exotics star-like shone.

And many another bed of flowers was there,
Inscribed with many a name well known to me,
And as I cast mine eyes around, I saw
The garden plot of one to whom men bowed
As to an image set upon an hill,
And lo! the ground was full of poisonous weeds;
And as I turn'd, upon the other side
Was one that bore a name which few men knew,
And fewer loved; and lo! the odorous earth
Blazed bright with colour, and the wandering
 breeze
Grew sweet with scent of violet and rose,
And fresh with bracing smells of heather-bloom.
And close beside mine own sad wilderness,
Yet sunder'd by the passage of a stream,
Was one that bore my lady's name, and here
The flowers were all disorder'd as mine own,
Yet where therein the stephanotis bloom'd,

A dark sweet-smelling herb was planted thick,
Whose dull green leaflets murmur'd like a harp
Whereon an angel plays.

   * * * * * *

         Thus each man's life
Is pictured in the flowers of Fairyland,
And oft when morning wakens into day,
And oft at dawn of night, I thither stray
As doth a sunlit cloud among the skies,
And all this life of ours becomes a dream,
A tale of talk and fancy;—but when earth
Comes back before mine eyes, the skies and flowers
Of Fairyland are distant as the stars,
And indistinct as thoughts of other days.
Yet somewhere in the meshes of the mind
There lies a knowledge, like a struggling gleam
Of light, which whispers inly to the soul,—
And then I know it is not all a dream.

THE SCALD'S DEATH-SONG.

SAD and cold from the strife
Lies the battle-crop grim,
Flashing gaily with life
Move the mail'd crowds from battle,
While soundeth the hymn.

Oh! joyous is life,
And oh! silent is death,
And oh! swift is the passing
Away of the breath.
As a flower that shuts
When the evening draws on,
So are all things that live,
They exist, then are gone.
As the ravens fly over
The field of the slain,
So hover the Fates

In the sky that broods lowering
O'er destiny's main.
And soon shall the harps
That so joyfully sound,
With the hands that awake them,
Be hush'd in the gloom
Of the funeral mound,
When the raven shall fly
Through the hush of the sky
O'er the dead.

The were-wolf is howling
In horrible glee,
The witch-wives are winging
O'er land and o'er sea
To the red field of slaughter,
Where sleepeth the brave,
The end of whose honour
Is naught but to lie
With the heaven for a grave.

The grave is the end
Of all glory and fame,
Of the deeds of the warrior,
The bard's sacred flame;
And the hush of the charnel

Is waiting for all,
And the end of all living
Is cerecloth and pall,
And the cold ring of stones
O'er the mouldering bones
Of the dead.

The face of the future
Is cloudy and dim,
With the mists of the shadows
That curtain-like veil it
In mysteries grim.
Life is sweet, life is short,
As the gleam of a fire
That flashes a moment
With brief lurid radiance
Before it expire.
Death is long, death is fearful,
Yet fleet as the storm
That walks o'er the waters
And lashes the waves
Into foam, comes his form.
And I hear and I see
That that form comes to me,
Riding wildly and fast
In the van of the blast;

And the night-wind shall sigh
O'er the desolate plain,
With death for its burden,
With silence for guerdon,
Of lips that now singing,
Of words that now winging,
Shall wake not again:
When the grey Evening star
Shall shine pale from afar
O'er the dead.

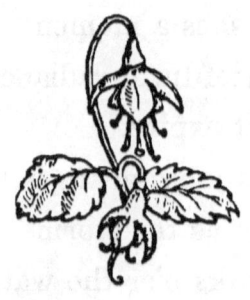

FINIS.

Πᾶς δ' ὀδυνηρὸς βίος ἀνθρώπων,
κοὐκ ἔστι πόνων ἀνάπαυσις·
ἀλλ' ὅ τι τοῦ ζῆν φίλτερον ἄλλο
σκότος ἀμπίσχων κρύπτει νεφέλαις.
δυσέρωτες δὴ φαινόμεθ' ὄντες
τοῦδ' ὅτι τοῦτο στίλβει κατὰ γῆν,
δι' ἀπειροσύνην ἄλλου βιότου
κοὐκ ἀπόδειξιν τῶν ὑπὸ γαίας.
    EURIPIDES, *Hippolytus*, 190-197.

ἐν τῷ φρονεῖν γὰρ μηδὲν ἥδιστος βίος,
[τὸ μὴ φρονεῖν γὰρ κάρτ' ἀνώδυνον κακόν,]
ἕως τὸ χαίρειν καὶ τὸ λυπεῖσθαι μάθῃς.
    SOPHOCLES, *Ajax*, 554-5.

IGHT closes in on the day, and the songs and the works of the daytime,
Swift from the splendour of morn flieth the gloom of the night :
There is an ending of all things on earth, of work and of playtime,
Ending of music and dance, ending of darkness and light;

Ending of summer and winter, of snows and of
    odour of roses,
  Everything comes to an end, long though it
    labour and sigh;
Seed into shadow of leaves, and bud into blossom
    uncloses,
  Bloom into promise of fruit, fruit that shall
    wither and die.
Thus in the flight of the days the hour of the verse's
    beginning
  Toils up the mountain of Time, steadily on to
    the end,
Peak after peak of the steep still warily, watch-
    fully winning,
  Up to the ultimate height whither its wanderings
    tend.
Thus have I started to climb, and now that my
    journey is ended,
  Foot on the summit, I gaze wistfully into the
    Past,
Scanning each turn of the pathway o'er which I
    have patiently wended,
  Up to the uttermost rock, up to the summit at
    last.
Is it for joy or for sorrow, that thus in the mist of
    the dawning,

FINIS.

Echoes of strains of the eve linger unwilling to die,
  Shadows and sounds of the night outlast in the brightness of morning,
    Dreamland melts into day, yet will not utterly fly?
Is there a pride in my heart as I look on the skein I have ravelled,
  Is there a light in mine eyes, bright as the beam of the sun,
Is it a pleasure to think of the paths and the ways I have travelled,
  Yea, is the longing appeased now that the labour is done?
Why, then, is my spirit oppress'd with the load of a pain that is double,
  Why is the peace of the soul further and further from me?
Oh! I could hide me from Time and its hate, and from Life and its trouble,
  Yea, on the bosom of night, yea, on the breast of the sea.
Oh! I could lie like a crystal of snow on the plain of the ocean,
  Cold in a passionless sleep, hidden away out of sight,

Far from the rush of the ice-wind of Memory that stirs into motion
  Myriads of ghosts of the gone, coffin'd and shrouded and white:
Hopes and illusions of old, so madly and tenderly cherished,
  Nurselings of wishes and fears, foster'd and tended with tears,
Loves of the days of my childhood, and loves of a youth that is perish'd,
  Stretch'd in the silence of space, laid upon limitless biers;
Sere as the hurrying leaves that the blast drives hither and thither,
  Empty as phantoms of air, blown with the touch of a breath,—
Oh! I could fly from the tortures of Sorrow, but whither, ah! whither?
  Where shall I flee from myself, where shall I rest but in death?
Yet I desire not death, for life is the season of working,
  Death is a sleep, and in death, none may put hand to the plough,
The grave is a terror besides, for we know not what shapes may lie lurking

Deep in its caves, we but know things that stand plain to us now.
Dim is our glimpse of the Future, and dim in the glare and the glitter,
The noise and bustle of life, flickers the flame of the soul,
The juice of the fruit of the tomb to the lips and the palate is bitter,
What shall the taste of it be, then, when we feast on it whole?
Shall it not be as the nectar of old, as the droppings of honey,
Strong to the heart and the brain, loaded with scent as of wine,
Clear as Nepenthe of lands where the vault of the heaven is sunny,
And the smile of a fortunate sky shines on the berry-clad vine?
Shall it not be as a vision, a sleep, a forgetting of sorrow,
A low monotonous song, lulling to Lethe of woe;
A promise of quietude marred by the wail of no poisonous to-morrow,
A valley of laughing flowers, fed by a fountainous flow?

Oh! for Elysium on earth! for wisdom though
    precious is mournful,
Heaviest burden is laid ever on soul that is
    strong,
Weeping the wise man goes, and while fools are
    lightsome and scornful,
Spirits of godliest mould hopelessly murmur,
    "How long?"—
And oft as we walk on our way, we behold in the
    stage-play of being
One with the soul of a god, trodden of feet like
    a sod,
And again as we look on the earth, we see, and
    are troubled in seeing,
One with the heart of a sod, worshipped of men
    as a god.
And the fate of the wise is as dark as the depth
    of a fathomless saying,
Culled from the Sibylline leaves, ages and ages
    ago;
And the fate of the poet is grief, and the verse of
    his lips is the playing,
Sad beyond measure, of Pain, harper that
    harpeth of woe:
And the flame of his fancy is fanned into blaze and
    to roar as of fire,

Fire that consumeth his brain, flame that
  devoureth his bones,—
Fanned by a breeze that destroys, yet awakens the
  agonized lyre,
And from the deathshriek of Joy, modulates
  marvellous tones ;
And the ear of the hearer is quick, as he listens
  in awe and in wonder,
Listens and longs for the gift, fearful yet lovely
  of song,
And knows not the voice is so sweet while the
  soul strings are bursting asunder,
Sees not the smoke, as the sparks rise in a
  luminous throng.
Toil is the portion of man, and toil is the harvest
  of toiling,
Wind of the whirlwind is reaped, foam of the
  forest of foam,—
Nay, it is useless to struggle and fret, what boots
  it recoiling ?
Cling to the ground, thou shalt grasp nothing
  but ashes and loam ;
Soar to the skies, thou shalt fall it may be, but
  even in falling,
Grander the grave of the great, better the
  loftier doom ;

Vile is the wreck of the hovel, the crash of the tower is appalling,
  Yea, though they both be as dust, hid in the house of the tomb.
Men may not love thee, yet work, and heed neither scorn nor derision,
  Work and thine honour shall live, death shall not sweep thee away,
Thou shalt become as a thought that is dear, as a beautiful vision,
  Long after worms of the ground die and return to their clay.
This is the end of the great, to soar ever higher and higher,
  Up to the cold height of heaven, up to the regions of snow ;
Freezing and bitter the air that surroundeth the souls that aspire,
  Yet shall they know and behold things never dreamt of below.
Mighty are these, and their words and their works are a garland of glory,
  Greener than laurels of fame bound on the brows of a king :
Yea, they shall live when the years of our time are a legend of story,

FINIS.

Writ in the page of the Past, fled like a fabulous thing.
These are the lips that are touched with a coal from the altar of fire,
These are the gold of the earth, purged in a furnace of pain,
Seven times sifted and tried and refined from the dross and the mire,
Brilliant and burnished as steel, perfect from blemish and stain.
These are the chosen of God, and the stamp of His seal is upon them,
These hath He set for Himself, girded with strength to the fight,
Given them breastplate and shield and helmet,— shall they not don them,
Struggle and strive and prevail, passing from might unto might?
Yea, though His hand presseth sore, yet His voice giveth strength to the weary,
Yea, they shall vanquish in fight, conquer and triumph at last,
Limbs may wax faint in the conflict, and soul may be clouded and dreary,
Yet shall they rest and be glad, then when the battle is past.

What though the spirit be crushed, and the day-dream of happiness faded,
    What though the love of the soul torture and prick like a goad,
What though the lamp of our life, and the smile of our sunshine be shaded,
Shall we not trust in our God, wait till He lighten our load?
Shall we not lean upon Him who sustaineth the weight of the ages,
    He whose one Law is divine, He whose one Purpose is love?
Shall we carp at the book of His will that know not one of its pages, —
    We who are earth of the earth murmur at what is above?
Nay, let us trust and be still, for the end shall excel the beginning,
    Wisdom is winnowed by woe, sorrowful singing is sweet;
Are there no wreaths of success, no prizes worthy the winning,
    Even though love, light, and joy, wither away at our feet?
Then let us press to the mark of the crown of our infinite calling,

Look not behind us nor stay, pause not by night
    or by day.
Waste not a moment in play, while the sand of our
    being is falling,
Minutes more precious than gems ghostily glid-
    ing away:
Let us not weep nor lament, but rejoice in the
    fulness of power,
Strong both to will and to do, stable and sted-
    fast of soul,
Spurning the lazy content of the world, and through
    tempest and shower
Worthily working our way, heedfully nearing
    our goal.
Thus shall we compass our end, not happy per-
    chance, but immortal,
Thus shall we finish our task, sigh forth our
    spirit and sleep,
Pass from the turmoil of Time to the hush of
    Eternity's portal,
And if our labour be long, shall not our slumber
    be deep?

CHISWICK PRESS:—PRINTED BY WHITTINGHAM AND WILKINS,
TOOKS COURT, CHANCERY LANE.

www.ingramcontent.com/pod-product-compliance
Lightning Source LLC
Chambersburg PA
CBHW020859230426
43666CB00008B/1246